DIVING DEEP:

Discovering God's Love Through Personal Scripture Study

Volume 1

Tramon Butts

Table of Contents

Introduction

Understanding the extensive nature of the full depth of God's love is not an instantaneous revelation; it is a lifelong pursuit. Each verse you study, each passage you ponder, and each promise you cling to reveals another facet of this divine affection. Through personal Bible study, you experience the breadth, the length, the height, and the depth of a love that surpasses all knowledge—a love that calls you by name and invites you into an eternal embrace.

For many, this book sits on a shelf, its edges gathering dust, its pages untouched. For some, it's a book visited during moments of need, sought out for guidance in times of turmoil. Yet, for the few who truly dive deep, taking the time to immerse themselves in its waters daily, it's a living testament to God's undying love, a guide to life's most profound truths.

The Bible isn't just a book; it's a conversation with the Almighty God. Each passage, each verse, each word carries with it a message, a lesson, a promise. But to merely read is not enough; one must engage, reflect, and apply. Personal Bible study is more than just reading; it's a deep, personal introspection, a communion with God, an exploration of one's soul through the lens of scripture.

It's easy to skim the surface, to take verses at face value. But God's love is profound, boundless, and multifaceted. Just as a gem reveals different colors and depths when turned under the light, so too does scripture unfold and deepen in meaning when applied personally. It's one thing to know that God loves humanity, but it's another to understand that He loves you, with all your flaws, dreams, and intricacies.

Applying the scriptures to personal experiences brings them to life. The stories aren't just tales of old; they become reflections of our own journeys. When we read about David's struggles, Esther's courage, or Paul's transformation, we see fragments of ourselves. We begin to grasp that these are not just historical figures but mirrors reflecting God's work in every human heart, including our own.

The importance of personal Bible study cannot be understated. It's the key to unlocking the depths of God's love. When you meditate on the Word, when you ask tough questions, when you challenge your beliefs and allow the scriptures to shape and mold you, you embark on a journey of discovery. And on this journey, you'll find that the more you understand the scriptures, the clearer the image becomes of a God whose love for you is deeper than the oceans, vaster than the skies, and more personal than you've ever imagined.

As you turn each page, may you find not just words, but whispers of love from the One who knows you best. Dive deep, dear reader, for in the depths, you'll discover a love that changes everything.

The Bible places a high value on personal study and understanding of God's Word. Numerous verses throughout the Old and New Testaments emphasize the importance of seeking knowledge, understanding, and wisdom, especially from the scriptures. Here are some passages that discuss or allude to the concept of personal study:

1. Joshua 1:8 - "This Book of the Law shall not depart from your mouth, but you shall meditate on it day and night, so that you may be careful to do according to all that is written in it. For then you will make your way prosperous, and then you will have good success."

2. Psalms 1:2 - "But his delight is in the law of the Lord, and on his law he meditates day and night."

3. Psalms 119:105 - "Your word is a lamp to my feet and a light to my path."

4. Proverbs 2:1-5 - "My son, if you receive my words and treasure up my commandments with you, making your ear attentive to wisdom and inclining your heart to understanding; yes, if you call out for insight and raise your voice for understanding, if you seek it like silver and search for it as for hidden treasures, then you will understand the fear of the Lord and find the knowledge of God."

5. Acts 17:11 - "Now the Berean Jews were of more noble character than those in Thessalonica, for they received the message with great eagerness and examined the Scriptures every day to see if what Paul said was true."

6. 2 Timothy 2:15 - "Do your best to present yourself to God as one approved, a worker who does not need to be ashamed and who correctly handles the word of truth."

7. 2 Timothy 3:16-17 - "All Scripture is breathed out by God and profitable for teaching, for reproof, for correction, and for

training in righteousness, that the man of God may be complete, equipped for every good work."

8. Hebrews 4:12 - "For the word of God is living and active, sharper than any two-edged sword, piercing to the division of soul and of spirit, of joints and of marrow, and discerning the thoughts and intentions of the heart."

The content that lies within this devotional is derived from expository sermons I have delivered over the years. It is through that reading and study that the Word breathe life into the pages herein. These passages, among others, indicate the value that the Bible places on personal study, reflection on its teachings, and striving for understanding. It encourages believers to immerse themselves in the scriptures, seek wisdom, and apply the lessons learned in their lives.

CHAPTER 1

Devotional: "For Best Results, Follow Instructions"

Scripture Reading: Acts 2:36-47; Matthew 28:18-20

Reflection: The Christian walk often feels like assembling a complex puzzle without the picture on the box. We know there's a beautiful image to create, but figuring out the placement of each piece can be daunting. How do we approach others about Jesus? How do we deepen our relationship with Him? Today's sermon reflects on the importance of following God's instructions to achieve His intended outcome in our lives.

Just as cooking a meal requires following steps in a specific sequence, our spiritual growth and the fulfillment of the Great Commission are no different. The heart of the instruction is simple yet profound – preach, speak, teach, and testify about Jesus. By focusing on Him and relying on the guidance of the Holy Spirit, the early church witnessed miracles and exponential growth.

We are reminded that repentance, baptism, and the acceptance of the Holy Spirit aren't checkboxes to salvation. Instead, they are expressions of our inward transformation.

The early church grew not just because they followed instructions, but because they lived out their faith collectively. Their unified commitment to God's teachings, fellowship, worship, and outreach serves as a blueprint for us today.

Takeaway: For the best outcome in our spiritual lives and in bringing others to Christ, we must lean on His instructions. By centering our lives around Jesus and living out our faith authentically, we become beacons of hope and vessels of His transformative power.

Study Questions:

1. **Reflecting on God's Instructions:** How do you currently incorporate the teachings of Jesus in your daily life? Are there areas where you feel you might be 'deviating from the instructions'?

2. **Testifying about Jesus:** Think about a time when sharing your experience with Jesus deeply impacted someone. If you haven't had such an experience, consider ways you can authentically share your faith journey with others.

3. **Unified in Devotion:** The early church was characterized by unity in devotion to God's teachings, fellowship, worship, and outreach. Which of these areas do you feel most drawn to, and how can you further invest in it?

4. **Repentance and Baptism:** How do you understand the relationship between repentance, baptism, and salvation? Why are these outward expressions important in our Christian journey?

5. **Living Authentically:** Acts 2:44-47 paints a picture of believers living out their faith publicly. How can you ensure that your faith is not just an internal belief but a public testimony?

As you ponder these questions, remember that the Christian journey is one of continuous growth. With every step, as you seek to align with God's instructions, you are being shaped into the vessel He desires, reflecting His glory to the world around.

Dive Deeper Daily:

Day 1: Introduction to the Importance of Instructions *Reading*: Acts 2:36-47

Reflection: Just as in practical day-to-day tasks, the importance of following God's instructions is paramount. When we deviate from the path He has set, we may end up with unintended outcomes or a longer journey than necessary. How have you experienced the results of not following God's instructions in your life?

Study Question:

1. How do the given examples of washing clothes, cooking, and assembling items relate to the spiritual importance of following instructions?

Day 2: The Great Commission *Reading*: Matthew 28:18-20

Reflection: Jesus has commissioned us to make disciples, teaching them to observe all His commands. Remember, He promises to be with us until the end of time. How are you living out the Great Commission in your life?

Study Questions:

1. How do different Bible translations enhance your understanding of the command to "make disciples"?

2. Why is it significant that Jesus assures us of His presence as we carry out His commission?

Day 3: Preaching Jesus *Reading*: Acts 2:22-24

Reflection: Peter's transformation from a fisherman to a disciple is a testament to God's power. He became a voice to people who knew about Jesus but had yet to acknowledge Him as Lord and Savior. In what ways has God transformed and used you to speak to others?

Study Questions:

1. What is the importance of emphasizing both the humanity and divinity of Jesus when sharing the gospel?

2. How does Peter address the responsibility of the Jews in Jesus' crucifixion?

Day 4: Conviction and Conversion *Reading*: Acts 2:37-39

Reflection: The true message of Jesus brings conviction to the heart. That prick, that feeling of being moved, signifies the Holy Spirit's work. Reflect on the moments when you felt convicted by God's word.

Study Questions:

1. Why do you think Peter's words had such a powerful effect on the people, leading them to ask, "What shall we do?"

2. What is the relationship between repentance, baptism, and faith?

Day 5: The Early Church and Its Foundations *Reading*: Acts 2:41-47

Reflection: The early church thrived on teaching, fellowship, worship, and evangelism. Reflect on the foundations of your local church. Are these four pillars evident in its practices?

Study Questions:

1. Why is the teaching of the apostles considered foundational to the early church's growth?

2. How did the early believers showcase their faith publicly, and how can we emulate their example today?

Day 6: Our Kingdom Assignment *Reading*: Ephesians 2:8-9; 1 Thessalonians 5:11

Reflection: We are saved by grace through faith. As members of God's family, we are to love, encourage, carry burdens, and forgive one another. Reflect on your role in God's kingdom and your relationship with other believers.

Study Questions:

1. How do the teachings from Ephesians and Thessalonians apply to our roles as disciples in the modern world?

2. In what ways can you foster deeper fellowship and unity within your church community?

Day 7: Conclusion – Living Out Our Devotion *Reading*: Galatians 6:2; John 15:12

Reflection: The power of the Holy Spirit can bring amazing transformations when the church is unified in devotion to God. Reflect on your personal journey and how you can further align with God's kingdom assignment.

Study Questions:

1. What does it mean to you to live out your faith publicly?

2. How can you actively participate in evangelism and not just leave it to church leaders?

May this devotional guide you deeper into understanding the importance of following God's instructions and living out the teachings of Jesus in your daily life. Amen.

CHAPTER 2

Devotional: "Blessed Assurance in the Shepherd's Embrace"

Scripture Reading: John 10:1-18

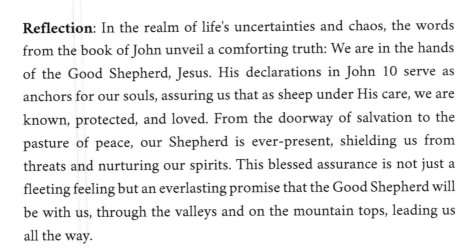

Reflection: In the realm of life's uncertainties and chaos, the words from the book of John unveil a comforting truth: We are in the hands of the Good Shepherd, Jesus. His declarations in John 10 serve as anchors for our souls, assuring us that as sheep under His care, we are known, protected, and loved. From the doorway of salvation to the pasture of peace, our Shepherd is ever-present, shielding us from threats and nurturing our spirits. This blessed assurance is not just a fleeting feeling but an everlasting promise that the Good Shepherd will be with us, through the valleys and on the mountain tops, leading us all the way.

Study Questions:

1. **Identity and Assurance**:

    - How does knowing that Jesus identifies Himself as the door give you confidence in your relationship with God?

- Reflect on a time when you truly felt like a sheep, lost and in need of guidance. How did you experience Jesus as your shepherd during that time?

2. **The Shepherd's Care:**

- What qualities of a good shepherd stand out to you the most from the passage? Why?

- How does the promise of Jesus laying down His life for the sheep increase your understanding of His love for you?

3. **Voice and Obedience:**

- Jesus mentions that His sheep hear His voice. How do you discern the voice of the Good Shepherd in your life?

- In what areas of your life do you need to better attune your ears to Jesus' voice and direction?

4. **Protection and Abundance:**

- How does the contrast of the thief (who comes to steal, kill, and destroy) with the shepherd (who gives abundant life) influence your understanding of spiritual warfare?

- Describe a time when you experienced the "abundant life" that Jesus promises. What did it look like for you?

5. **Restoration and Compassion:**

- Reflecting on the image of the cast sheep, can you identify moments in your life when you felt 'cast down' and in need of Jesus' restoration?

- How can we, as the body of Christ, embody the role of a shepherd to others who are "cast down" or wandering away from the fold?

6. **The One-Fold and Unity**:

- Jesus speaks of other sheep that are not of the current fold. How does this verse challenge or broaden your understanding of God's inclusiveness and mission?

- In what ways can you contribute to fostering unity among believers and drawing others into the one-fold of Jesus?

Closing Prayer: Dear Heavenly Father, thank You for the blessed assurance we have in Jesus, our Good Shepherd. In the midst of life's trials and uncertainties, may we cling to the truth that we are known, protected, and loved by You. Help us to hear Your voice clearly and follow Your leading every day. Restore us when we're cast down and guide us into the abundant life You promise. In Jesus' name, we pray, Amen.

Dive Deeper Daily:

Day 1: Scripture: John 10:7 *"Then said Jesus unto them again, Verily, verily, I say unto you, I am the door of the sheep."*

Reflection: Jesus is our point of access to the Kingdom. He is the protector who grants us entry into His flock. Just as a door provides security, Jesus provides a protective covering over our lives.

Study Questions:

1. What does it mean to you personally that Jesus is the door?

2. How does knowing Jesus as our "door" provide you with a sense of assurance?

Day 2: Scripture: John 10:9 *"I am the door: by me if any man enter in, he shall be saved, and shall go in and out, and find pasture."*

Reflection: Through Jesus, we find nourishment, protection, and the peace that surpasses understanding. As our guide, He ensures we never stray too far from His path.

Study Questions:

1. How has Jesus led you to "green pastures" in your life?

2. What does it mean to "go in and out" with Jesus?

Day 3: Scripture: John 10:10 *"The thief cometh not, but for to steal, and to kill, and to destroy: I am come that they might have life, and that they might have it more abundantly."*

Reflection: Jesus contrasts Himself with the forces of darkness. While thieves bring destruction, Jesus offers a rich, fulfilling life.

Study Questions:

1. How do you discern the difference between the voice of the thief and the voice of the Shepherd?

2. In what ways has Jesus given you abundant life?

Day 4: Scripture: John 10:11 *"I am the good shepherd: the good shepherd giveth his life for the sheep."*

Reflection: Jesus, the Shepherd, sacrificed Himself out of love for us. His commitment is a testament to His character and love.

Study Questions:

1. How does it feel knowing Jesus, as the Good Shepherd, gave His life for you?

2. What are some ways you can emulate the love of the Good Shepherd in your daily life?

Day 5: Scripture: John 10:12 *"But he that is an hireling, and not the shepherd, whose own the sheep are not, seeth the wolf coming, and leaveth the sheep, and fleeth: and the wolf catcheth them, and scattereth the sheep."*

Reflection: We can't place our trust solely in worldly things. Only Jesus remains faithful, even in our times of peril.

Study Questions:

1. Can you recall a time when you placed trust in something or someone other than Jesus and were let down?

2. How does the steadfastness of Jesus increase your faith and assurance in Him?

Day 6: Scripture: John 10:14 *"I am the good shepherd, and know my sheep, and am known of mine."*

Reflection: To be known by Jesus is to be loved, cherished, and protected. It is a personal relationship, where we recognize His voice and follow His lead.

Study Questions:

1. What comfort do you draw from knowing that Jesus knows you personally?

2. How can you deepen your relationship with the Good Shepherd?

Day 7: Scripture: John 10:16 *"And other sheep I have, which are not of this fold: them also I must bring, and they shall hear my voice; and there shall be one fold, and one shepherd."*

Reflection: Jesus is the universal Shepherd. His love isn't limited by boundaries. He seeks to unite all under His care, demonstrating an inclusive love.

Study Questions:

1. How can you help in bringing others to hear the voice of the Shepherd?

2. What steps can you take to be more inclusive and loving like Jesus?

CHAPTER 3

Devotional on Blessed Assurance – Part II

Scripture Reading: Psalm 23

Reflection: Today's scripture reading took us on a journey through Psalm 23, a beloved scripture that many can recite by heart. We explored the depth and richness of the relationship between the Shepherd and His sheep. The story of the actor and the young man was a poignant reminder that knowing about God is different from truly knowing God.

Story Illustration: There was once an actor who was known everywhere for his one-man show of readings and recitations from the classics. He would always end his performance with a dramatic reading of Psalm 23. Each night, without exception, as the actor began his recitation-"The Lord is my shepherd, I shall not want"-the crowd would listen attentively. And then, at the conclusion of the psalm, they would rise in thunderous applause in appreciation of the actor's incredible ability to bring the verse to life.

But one night, just before the actor was to offer his customary recital of Psalm 23, a young man from the audience spoke up. "Sir do you mind if tonight I recite Psalm 23? "The actor was quite taken back by this unusual request, but he allowed the young man to come forward and stand front and center on the stage to recite the psalm, knowing that the ability of this unskilled youth would be no match for his own talent.

With a soft voice, the young man began to recite the words of the psalm. When he was finished, there was no applause. There was no standing ovation as on other nights. All that could be heard was the sound of weeping.

The audience had been so moved by the young man's recitation that every eye was full of tears. Amazed by what he had heard, the actor said to the youth, "I don't understand. I have been performing Psalm 23 for years. I have a lifetime of experience and training, but I have never been able to move an audience as you have tonight. Tell me, what is your secret?

"The young man humbly replied, "Well sir, you know the psalm... but I know the Shepherd."

Study Questions:

1. **Personal Relationship with the Shepherd:** The young man in the story was profoundly impactful in his recitation of Psalm 23 because he knew the Shepherd. Reflect on your own relationship with the Lord. Do you feel you know about Him or truly know Him?

2. **Jehovah in Psalm 23:** Each verse of Psalm 23 associates the Lord with a different name that describes His character. For instance, Jehovah-Jireh refers to the Lord as our Provider. Which of these names resonate with you the most right now and why?

3. **Want vs. Need:** The sermon differentiates between our wants and our needs, and how sometimes our wants can pull us away from God. Can you identify a time in your life when a want distracted you from what was truly important?

4. **Rest in Him:** Psalm 23:2 speaks of the Lord making us lie down in green pastures and leading us beside still waters. Reflect on the last time you truly rested in God, letting go of all your worries and stressors. What did that feel like? If it's been a while, what's holding you back?

5. **God in Control:** The sermon emphasizes that God is in control of our lives. What area of your life do you need to surrender to Him today, trusting that He "got this"?

6. **Restoration:** Psalm 23:3 mentions the Lord restoring our souls. Share a time when you felt spiritually drained or distant from God and experienced His restoration.

7. **Blessed Assurance:** Throughout the sermon, we're reminded of the Blessed Assurance we have in Christ. How does understanding that Jesus is our Shepherd, Protector, Guide, Comfort, and so much more, influence your day-to-day decisions and feelings?

Prayer: Lord, thank You for being our Shepherd, for knowing us intimately, and for always providing for our needs. Help us to differentiate between our wants and our true needs, and guide us to lean into You for our fulfillment. Grant us the blessed assurance of Your presence, control, and restoration in our lives. Amen.

Dive Deeper Daily:

Day 1: Knowing the Shepherd

Reading: Psalm 23:1 "The Lord is my shepherd; I shall not want."

Devotional: It's one thing to know about the Shepherd and quite another to truly know the Shepherd. When our understanding moves from mere knowledge to intimate experience, our perspective shifts. The actor knew the Psalm, but the young man knew the Shepherd. This makes all the difference in how we navigate life's challenges.

Study Questions:

1. Have there been moments in your life where you've felt a deeper connection to God as your Shepherd?

2. In what ways can you cultivate a closer relationship with the Shepherd?

3. Reflect on times when you've relied on mere knowledge versus an intimate understanding. How did those situations differ?

Day 2: The Lord - More than Just a Name

Reading: Psalm 23:1-3

Devotional: Names carry meaning, and the various names of God in Psalm 23 reveal His character and the many roles He plays in our lives. From Jehovah-Raah (Our Shepherd) to Jehovah-Shalom (Our Peace), these names paint a picture of a God who is not distant but actively involved in every aspect of our lives.

Study Questions:

1. Which name of God resonates with you the most currently and why?

2. How have you experienced Jehovah-Jireh (The Lord, my Provider) in your life?

3. Why is it important to recognize and call on God by His various names?

Day 3: The Shepherd's Assurance

Reading: Psalm 23:1-3

Devotional: David's words reflect a deep assurance in the care of the Lord, our Shepherd. Just as sheep are entirely dependent on their shepherd, so too are we dependent on the Lord. No matter our titles or achievements, we are all in need of God's guiding hand.

Study Questions:

1. Reflect on times when you felt God's guidance most clearly in your life.

2. What challenges or roles in your life have made you recognize your dependence on God?

3. How does understanding our dependence on God affect our daily decisions and actions?

Day 4: Navigating Wants and Needs

Reading: Psalm 23:1

Devotional: Our society often blurs the line between wants and needs. David's declaration that with the Lord as his Shepherd, he shall not want, reminds us that God provides all our needs. When we align our desires with God's will, our wants become reflections of our true needs.

Study Questions:

1. List down some 'wants' you've mistaken for 'needs' recently. Reflect on why this might be.

2. How can you discern between genuine needs and mere wants?

3. How has God provided for your needs in the past?

Day 5: Embracing God's Control

Reading: Psalm 23:2-3

Devotional: In a world that encourages self-sufficiency, recognizing and embracing God's control can be countercultural. However, when we surrender control to God, the One who makes, leads, and restores, we find true peace and assurance.

Study Questions:

1. In what areas of your life are you struggling to surrender control to God?

2. Reflect on the action words in Psalm 23:2-3. How do they paint a picture of God's care and guidance?

3. Share a personal experience when surrendering control led to unexpected blessings.

Reflection: Throughout this week, as you meditate on Psalm 23, ask God to deepen your understanding of Him as your Shepherd. Let His assurance guide and comfort you in all circumstances.

Prayer: Lord, our Shepherd, guide us into a deeper understanding of Your love and care. Help us to trust You more, knowing that in Your hands, we shall not want. Amen.

CHAPTER 4

Devotional: The Assurance in Every Valley

Scripture Reading: Psalm 23:4-6

Devotional: In life, there are highs and lows, moments of jubilation, and stretches of despair. But in every twist and turn, Psalm 23 assures us of God's unending love, provision, and guidance. The valleys might be inevitable, but so is God's comforting presence. He isn't just watching us from a distance but walking alongside us every step of the way. The presence of a shadow implies the existence of light. So, even in our darkest moments, the Light of the World, Jesus Christ, is shining brightly, guiding us and offering hope. His rod and staff are symbols of His protection, guiding us away from danger and pulling us back when we stray. The overflowing cup in verse 5 is a reminder that God's blessings aren't just enough—they're abundant. And just like the newspaper reporter who followed the old pastor, God's goodness and mercy are always trailing us, ready to aid when we need it.

Reflection and Study Questions:

1. **Valleys as Faith Builders:** Think of a valley experience in your life. How did it help deepen your relationship with God? Did it strengthen your faith?

2. **Presence of Light:** In moments of darkness, have you tried looking for the "light"? Can you recall a moment when God's presence became clear during a trial?

3. **Fear Not:** What fears are you currently holding onto? How can the reminder that God is with you help alleviate those fears?

4. **You Are Not Alone:** Have there been times you felt alone? How does the assurance of God's constant presence change your perspective on those moments?

5. **God's Protection and Provision:** Think about a time when you witnessed God's protection or provision firsthand. How did that experience shape your understanding of Psalm 23:5?

6. **Reconciliation with Enemies:** Consider the line about the table prepared in the presence of enemies. Have you ever experienced reconciliation that you didn't expect? How can you approach situations with hope for reconciliation in the future?

7. **Goodness and Mercy:** In what ways have you experienced God's goodness and mercy recently? How can you be more aware of these blessings in your daily life?

Close in prayer, thanking God for His blessed assurance, protection, and abundant blessings. Ask Him for the strength and faith to keep moving, especially in the valleys, and the eyes to see His light even in the darkest shadows.

Dive Deeper Daily:

Day 1:

Scripture Reading: Psalm 23:4

Devotional Thought: As we walk through life's valleys, we need not fear. Our Shepherd is with us, leading, guiding, and protecting us.

Study Questions:

1. Reflect on a recent valley experience in your life. How did you feel God's presence during that time?

2. How does the imagery of the shepherd's rod and staff provide comfort for you?

Day 2:

Scripture Reading: John 16:33

Devotional Thought: Valleys in life are inevitable, but our Savior has overcome the world.

Study Questions:

1. How does it comfort you to know that Jesus has overcome the world?

2. Share an instance when you've experienced peace amidst a trial because of your faith.

Day 3:

Scripture Reading: James 4:14

Devotional Thought: Life can be unpredictable, but with God leading us, we can be prepared for any valley.

Study Questions:

1. Why is it important to recognize the unpredictability of life?

2. How can we ensure we're spiritually prepared for life's valleys?

Day 4:

Scripture Reading: Matthew 5:45

Devotional Thought: God's love and provision are consistent, even in the valleys. He ensures the sun rises for all, showing His impartiality.

Study Questions:

1. How do you reconcile God's love for all with the presence of suffering?

2. Reflect on a time when you saw God's provision during a challenging period.

Day 5:

Scripture Reading: 1 Peter 1:6

Devotional Thought: Even though valleys may seem prolonged, they are only temporary. Trust in God's timing.

Study Questions:

1. How can recognizing the temporariness of trials change our perspective?

2. Why is patience essential in enduring valleys?

Day 6:

Scripture Reading: Psalm 23:5

Devotional Thought: God's provision, even amidst enemies and obstacles, is a testament to His unfailing love.

Study Questions:

1. How have you seen God prepare a table for you amidst adversity?

2. Reflect on God's abundance in your life. How has your "cup runneth over"?

Day 7:

Scripture Reading: Hebrews 13:5

Devotional Thought: We are never alone in our journey. God's promise to never leave us provides blessed assurance.

Study Questions:

1. Recall a moment when you felt God's undeniable presence.

2. How can we continually remind ourselves of God's ever-present nature in our lives?

Closing Prayer:

Heavenly Father, we thank You for the Blessed Assurance we have in You. As we walk through the valleys of life, help us remember that You are with us, guiding, comforting, and providing for us. May we always find solace in Your word, and let the knowledge of Your presence be the light that guides us. In Jesus' name, we pray. Amen.

CHAPTER 5

Devotional: There's a Doctor in Town that I Highly Recommend

Scripture Reading: Mark 6:52-56

Reflection: At times, the weight of our circumstances can blind us to the miracles unfolding before us. As we encounter challenges, we may feel overwhelmed, causing our focus to shift away from what Jesus has done and continues to do for us. But as we journey through life, we're reminded that Jesus is not just a historical figure but an ever-present force who heals, restores, and empowers us.

1. **Don't Forget What He's Already Done (v.52-53)**: Think back on the times when you felt all hope was lost, yet you experienced an unexpected breakthrough. Perhaps it was a job opportunity after months of unemployment, or healing after a prolonged illness. These moments, like the miracle of the loaves, remind us of the transformative power of Jesus. By recounting our blessings, we

fortify our faith, making it easier to trust Jesus in our current circumstances.

2. **Will You Recognize Him When He Shows Up? (v.54):** Familiarity can often make us complacent. The disciples, despite witnessing several miracles, failed to recognize Jesus during a storm. Similarly, we might overlook Jesus's presence in our lives, especially during challenging times. But, when we actively seek Him, we'll find Him showing up in unexpected ways.

3. **Have You Brought Anybody to Him? (v.55):** Our testimonies have the power to transform lives. When we share our encounters with Jesus, we become a beacon of hope to others, directing them to the ultimate source of healing and salvation.

4. **Embrace The Healing Touch (v.56):** Jesus offers complete restoration to those who seek Him. Just as the people believed that touching the hem of His garment would heal them, our faith in His ability to transform our lives can result in miracles.

Prayer: Lord Jesus, open our eyes to recognize Your constant presence and work in our lives. May we never forget the miracles You've performed for us. Equip us to share our testimonies, leading others to experience Your transformative touch. Amen.

Study Questions:

1. Reflect on a personal "miracle of the loaves" moment in your life when you experienced God's provision unexpectedly. How did it strengthen your faith?

2. In what areas of your life do you struggle to recognize Jesus's presence? What steps can you take to actively seek Him during challenging times?

3. How has someone else's testimony positively impacted your faith journey? How can you share your encounters with Jesus to bless others?

4. The people sought Jesus to touch the border of His garment and be healed. How does this highlight the importance of faith in experiencing God's healing?

5. How can you introduce others to the "Doctor in town" you highly recommend? List practical ways to compel others to experience Jesus's healing touch.

Dive Deeper Daily:

Day 1: Remembering Past Miracles

Scripture: Mark 6:52

Reflection: In our lives, it's so easy to forget the blessings and miracles that God has already done for us. Today, take a moment to recount those times when God showed up in unexpected ways.

Study Questions:

1. What miracles have you experienced in your life?

2. Why do you think the disciples forgot the miracle of the loaves?

3. How can you keep the memory of God's miracles fresh in your heart and mind?

Day 2: Recognizing Him in the Storm

Scripture: Mark 6:54

Reflection: Sometimes, we are so consumed by our challenges that we fail to recognize God's presence. Yet, He is always there, waiting for us to turn to Him.

Study Questions:

1. Have there been moments you failed to recognize God's intervention?

2. What distractions or worries prevent you from seeing God's hand in your life?

3. How can you better train your heart to recognize Him in every situation?

Day 3: Sharing Testimonies

Scripture: Mark 6:55

Reflection: Our personal experiences with God have the power to draw others closer to Him. By sharing our testimonies, we light the way for others.

Study Questions:

1. What is one testimony you can share with someone today?

2. How have others' testimonies impacted your faith journey?

3. How can you be more intentional about sharing what God has done in your life?

Day 4: Bringing Others to Him

Scripture: Mark 6:56

Reflection: Sometimes, the best way to introduce someone to Jesus is by inviting them to experience Him firsthand.

Study Questions:

1. Who in your life needs an introduction to Jesus?

2. What are some practical ways you can bring them closer to Him?

3. How does it feel knowing that your actions could potentially change someone's eternal destiny?

Day 5: Embracing the Ultimate Healer

Reflection: There are many healers in the world, but only one offers spiritual healing with eternal implications. As believers, we have the privilege of knowing and introducing others to the Great Physician.

Study Questions:

1. How has Jesus brought healing to your life?

2. In what areas do you still seek His healing touch?

3. How can you share about this ultimate healer with others?

Closing Prayer:

Heavenly Father, thank You for the miracles, both big and small, that You perform in our lives every day. Help us not to forget Your mighty works and to always recognize You, especially during our trials. May our testimonies draw others to You, and may we never hesitate to bring the sick, lost, and hurting to the feet of the Great Physician. We thank You for the assurance that comes with knowing Jesus, the doctor we can wholly recommend. In Jesus' name, Amen.

CHAPTER 6

Devotional: "The Journey of Humility, Desperation, and Faith"

Scripture Reading: James 4:10

Reflection: In life, we are often faced with trials that seem insurmountable. But through the story of Jairus, we learn the value of humility, desperation, and faith in the face of adversity. Jairus, a man of power and position, humbly approached Jesus, acknowledging Him as the ultimate authority. He displayed sheer desperation as he sought healing for his dying daughter. This desperation wasn't driven by hopelessness but by a firm faith that Jesus was the answer.

Jairus' journey mirrors the trials we face in life. Sometimes, just as we think we're about to receive our miracle, another situation arises, testing our patience and faith. But through the story, we're reminded to hold on, for help is on the way. Even when our situation appears dead, with faith, we can see it as merely "asleep", waiting for the touch of Jesus.

Reflection Questions:

1. **Humility**: Reflect on a time you set aside your pride and humbly approached God. What drove you to do so, and how did God respond?

2. **Desperation**: Have you ever been in a situation where you felt desperate for God's intervention? How did you handle the wait?

3. **Anticipation & Waiting**: How do you usually handle delays, especially when you see others receiving their blessings? How can you cultivate patience and trust during these times?

4. **Manifestation**: Can you recall a time when you saw God's hand move in a situation you had prayed about? How did it strengthen your faith?

Prayer:

Dear Heavenly Father, thank You for reminding us of the power of humility, desperation, and faith through Jairus' story. Help us to trust in Your timing, knowing that even when things seem dead, You can breathe life into them. Strengthen our faith and patience, especially during the waiting periods. We thank You for the testimonies we have and the ones yet to come, for we know that help is always on the way. In Jesus' name, we pray. Amen.

Dive Deeper Daily:

Scripture Reading: Mark 5:21-42

Devotional Thought: In our moments of despair and desperation, when it feels like the weight of the world is upon us, there is always hope in Jesus. Jairus, a man of stature and influence, was desperate. Despite his position, he found himself in need, unable to change the dire circumstances surrounding his dying daughter. But in his desperation, he turned to Jesus, understanding the power and authority of Christ. Similarly, we too can turn to Jesus in our moments of need, knowing that our cries do not go unheard.

Prayer: Lord Jesus, in our moments of desperation, help us to turn to you. Remind us that no situation is too big for you to handle and that you are always on time. Strengthen our faith and remind us that even when things seem bleak, you are always with us. Amen.

Study Questions:

1. Why do you think Jairus, a man of such high position, chose to humble himself before Jesus?

2. The woman with the issue of blood and Jairus's daughter are intertwined in this scripture. What similarities and differences can you identify in their stories?

3. In times of desperation, why do you think some people struggle to turn to Jesus?

4. How can waiting on God's timing instead of our own benefit us in the long run?

5. How do you personally handle situations when you feel God isn't answering your prayers or isn't moving fast enough?

Reflection: Think about a time when you felt desperate or in need of a breakthrough. How did you handle the situation? Were you able to find peace and trust in God's timing? If not, what held you back?

Action Step: Today, intentionally spend time in prayer, laying all your worries and concerns at the feet of Jesus. Trust that He hears you and is always on time. If possible, share a testimony with someone about a time God came through for you, reminding them that help is always on the way.

CHAPTER 7

Devotional: "The Congregation of Ungrateful Complainers"

Scripture Reading: Numbers 11:1-25

Reflection: Life is filled with challenges and struggles, but it is also adorned with blessings and victories. Complaining can often become a default reaction when faced with hardships, but God calls us to a life of gratitude. The Israelites, despite being provided for, fell into the trap of complaining, revealing an ungrateful heart. As believers, we must learn to see God's hand at work even in the toughest moments and choose gratitude over complaint.

Devotional Points:

1. **Remember God's Faithfulness**: God delivered the Israelites from the bondage of Egypt. Yet, they quickly forgot His miracles and grumbled about their present circumstances. Remembering what God has done for us in the past can fuel our gratitude in the present.

2. **Praise God in Every Situation**: Rather than reminiscing about the past, believers are encouraged to praise God in their current circumstances. Every situation provides an opportunity to witness God's provisions and blessings.

3. **Look Forward with Hope**: God's promises are true and He assures a future for His children. As believers, we hold on to the hope of eternal life with Christ, a place without pain or suffering.

Reflection & Study Questions:

1. In what situations do you find yourself complaining the most?

2. Recall a time when God's provision in your life was evident. How did that make you feel?

3. How can you cultivate a heart of gratitude even when facing challenges?

4. How does an attitude of gratitude influence those around you, especially non-believers?

5. Reflect on Romans 8:18. How does focusing on the eternal perspective change your view of current sufferings?

Prayer: Lord, help me to always remember Your faithfulness and love. Teach me to have a heart of gratitude in every situation, recognizing Your hand at work in my life. May my life be a testament to Your goodness, and may I always choose gratitude over complaint. Amen.

Action Steps:

1. Start a gratitude journal. Every day, write down at least three things you're thankful for.

2. Take a moment each day to thank God for His blessings, both big and small.

3. Encourage someone today. Share with them a time when God provided for you or showed His faithfulness.

Further Reading:

1 Thessalonians 5:18 – "Give thanks in all circumstances; for this is the will of God in Christ Jesus for you."

Philippians 4:6 – "Do not be anxious about anything, but in every situation, by prayer and petition, with thanksgiving, present your requests to God."

Colossians 3:15 – "Let the peace of Christ rule in your hearts, to which indeed you were called in one body. And be thankful."

Dive Deeper Daily:

Scripture: Numbers 11:1-25

Day 1: Reflection on God's Anger Toward Complaining

Read: Numbers 11:1-3

Reflection: Just like the Israelites, our ingratitude and complaints also displease God. Take a moment today to acknowledge any areas of your life where you may have been ungrateful.

Study Question: Why do you think God had such a strong reaction to the Israelites' complaining?

Day 2: God's Provision in the Past

Read: Numbers 11:4-6

Reflection: Remember times in the past when God has provided and been faithful, even when you didn't recognize it.

Study Question: What does remembering God's past faithfulness do for your present faith?

Day 3: God's Presence in the Present

Read: Numbers 11:9-10

Reflection: Even in our moments of discontent, God continues to provide. Reflect on His daily provisions in your life.

Study Question: How can acknowledging daily blessings help combat the tendency to complain?

Day 4: The Weight of Leadership

Read: Numbers 11:10-15

Reflection: Leadership comes with its challenges. Pray for your leaders, knowing that they carry heavy burdens at times.

Study Question: How does Moses' reaction to the people's complaints shed light on the responsibilities and pressures of leadership?

Day 5: Embracing Help in Leadership

Read: Numbers 11:16-17

Reflection: Leaders aren't meant to do everything alone. Reflect on ways you can support or be supported in leadership roles.

Study Question: How did God provide for Moses when he felt overwhelmed by his leadership responsibilities?

Day 6: The Danger of Ingratitude

Read: Numbers 11:18-20

Reflection: Continuous complaining can lead to consequences we might not desire. Take time to express gratitude for what you have, both big and small.

Study Question: What are the consequences of continually focusing on what we don't have rather than what God has already provided?

Day 7: A Heart of Gratitude

Reflection: Romans 8:18 reminds us of the hope we have in Christ. Praise God today for the future He has secured for you.

Study Question: How can focusing on the eternal promise of God help you remain grateful even in challenging times?

Closing Prayer: Lord, help us cultivate a heart of gratitude, remembering your faithfulness in the past, your provisions in the present, and the glorious future you've promised. Teach us to trust in You and to be content in all circumstances. Amen.

CHAPTER 8

Devotional: "A Blueprint for Prayer"

Scripture Reading: Matthew 6:9-13

Reflection: In today's busy world, we often find ourselves caught up in our daily routines, forgetting to take a moment to connect with our Heavenly Father. We sometimes struggle to find the right words or feel guilty about our infrequent communication. Yet, in His immense grace and wisdom, Jesus left us a blueprint – the Lord's Prayer.

In this simple yet profound prayer, Jesus reveals a structured approach to connect with the God of the universe. We are not merely talking to a distant deity but to "Our Father," one who desires relationship and connection. This relationship is the foundation of our prayers, reminding us that we approach God not based on our own righteousness but because of Jesus' righteousness.

Jesus teaches us that before we ask for anything, we should acknowledge who God is. By saying, "Our Father which art in heaven,

Hallowed be thy name," we prioritize God's honor and glory. We recognize that God's will is perfect and pray for it to manifest "on earth as it is in heaven."

Today, let's embrace this blueprint, not just as a ritual but as a heartfelt connection, trusting that our Father hears, understands, and responds.

Study Questions:

1. **Reflection:** When was the last time you felt deeply connected to God during prayer? What made that moment special?

2. **Understanding:** How does addressing God as "Our Father" change our perspective when we pray?

3. **Application:** How can you prioritize God's honor and glory in your daily life, outside of prayer?

4. **Insight:** In the sermon, the pastor mentions that we should trust God's will even if we don't understand it. Can you recall a time when God's will was different from yours, but it led to a positive outcome?

5. **Action:** Practice praying the Lord's Prayer daily, pausing after each line to meditate on its meaning. How does this deepen your connection with God?

6. **Discussion:** Jesus instructs us to pray, "Thy kingdom come, Thy will be done." How does this instruction align with the way we often approach God with our own wants and needs?

7. **Personal Reflection:** In your prayers, do you find yourself asking more or acknowledging and worshiping God more? What changes can you implement in your prayer life to find a balance?

Remember, prayer is our direct line to God, the ultimate source, sustainer, and supplier. Let's use this gift daily to foster a deeper relationship with Him.

Dive Deeper Daily:

Day 1: The Essence of Prayer

Scripture: Matthew 6:9a

Reflection: Understanding the significance of prayer, Jesus presents a model for us to approach God in the most authentic way. Before we rush into our requests, it's vital to recognize the one we're addressing: Our Father. This is not just about relationship but also about authority. When we say "Our Father," we are both connecting personally and acknowledging the ultimate authority.

Study Questions:

1. Why do you think it's important to recognize God's authority before making our requests?

2. How can understanding God's position as the "source, sustainer, supplier" deepen our trust in Him?

Day 2: Reverencing the Name of God

Scripture: Matthew 6:9b

Reflection: God's name is holy, distinctive, and unmatched. In approaching God, it's paramount to honor and reverence His name. Recognizing His character purifies our intentions and molds our requests.

Study Questions:

1. How does knowing the holiness of God's name affect how you approach Him in prayer?

2. In what ways can you show reverence to God daily?

Day 3: Aligning with God's Will

Scripture: Matthew 6:10

Reflection: "Thy Kingdom come, Thy will be done." In prayer, we are not just asking for our will but seeking alignment with God's will. It's a submission, a surrender, recognizing that God's plans are far superior to ours.

Study Questions:

1. How can you discern if what you're praying for aligns with God's will?

2. Why is it essential to prioritize God's will over our desires?

Day 4: Worship in Prayer

Scripture: Reflection on Matthew 6:9-10

Reflection: Prayer isn't merely about requests; it's also about worship. Heaven is a place of continual worship, and if we are to bring heaven's will to earth, we must become people of worship here and now.

Study Questions:

1. How can you incorporate worship into your daily prayer life?

2. Why is worship an essential component of effective prayer?

Day 5: The Trust in His Will

Scripture: Reflection on Matthew 6:10

Reflection: Trusting in God's will means having the confidence that God's plans for us are perfect, even if they're not always clear. By trusting Him, we acknowledge His infinite wisdom and boundless resources.

Study Questions:

1. Can you recall a time when God's will differed from yours, but later you realized it was for the best?

2. How can you cultivate a heart that says, "Let Your will be done" even in challenging times?

Day 6: Heaven as the Standard

Scripture: Reflection on Matthew 6:10

Reflection: Heaven is the epitome of God's perfection. When we pray, "on earth as it is in heaven," we're asking for a touch of that perfection here on earth. We're also reminded to continually strive for God's standard in our lives.

Study Questions:

1. How does comparing your life to heaven's standard help you in your spiritual growth?

2. What aspects of heaven do you most desire to experience on earth?

Day 7: Approaching God with Humility

Scripture: Overview of Matthew 6:9-13

Reflection: The model prayer that Jesus taught is wrapped in humility. Before asking for daily bread or forgiveness, it centers on recognizing who God is and aligning with His will. Humility in prayer prepares our hearts to receive from God.

Study Questions:

1. Why is humility crucial in prayer?

2. In what areas of your life can you practice more humility as you approach God?

Each day's devotional is meant to inspire deeper reflection on prayer's essence and guide believers in drawing closer to God through the model that Jesus provided.

CHAPTER 9

Devotional: Praying for We, Not Just Me

Scripture Reading: Matthew 6:9-13

Reflection: Jesus, during His Sermon on the Mount, didn't simply offer guidelines on how to pray; He provided a transformative model, emphasizing collective unity and interdependence. Through the Lord's Prayer, we're reminded to shift our focus from our isolated needs to the collective well-being of the community. When we pray "Give us this day our daily bread," we're not only seeking provision for ourselves but also for our brothers and sisters in Christ. Furthermore, forgiveness is as essential as our daily sustenance. Just as we crave our daily bread, our souls long for the daily absolution of our transgressions. But this cleansing also demands that we extend the same mercy to others, fostering a communal bond that echoes God's boundless love.

Key Verses:

- Matthew 6:11 - "Give us this day our daily bread."

- Matthew 6:12 - "And forgive us our debts, as we also have forgiven our debtors."

Study Questions:

1. **Reflecting on the Lord's Prayer:** Why do you think Jesus emphasized the collective terms like "us" and "our" instead of individualistic terms in the Lord's Prayer?

2. **The Role of Forgiveness:** Considering Matthew 6:12, why do you think Jesus links our plea for forgiveness with our willingness to forgive others?

3. **Remembrance of Provisions:** Reflect on the Israelites in the wilderness and how God provided them with daily manna. How can this story encourage you to trust God's daily provision in your life?

4. **Embracing Daily Dependence:** Why do you think Jesus encourages believers to ask for daily bread instead of monthly or yearly provisions? What does this teach us about our relationship and dependence on God?

5. **The Power of Forgiveness:** Drawing from Matthew 5:23-24, discuss the importance of reconciling with others before offering our gifts to God. How does unforgiveness obstruct our relationship with God?

6. **Emulating Christ's Forgiveness:** Reflect on Luke 6:27-28 and Matthew 18:21-22. How can you actively practice forgiveness in your daily life, even when it's challenging?

7. **Personal Reflection:** Think about the times you've found it difficult to pray for collective needs over personal ones. How can embracing the Lord's Prayer's model reshape your approach to intercessory prayer?

Prayer: Heavenly Father, thank You for teaching us the way we ought to pray. May we always remember the collective spirit of the Lord's Prayer, seeking not only for our needs but also for those of our brothers and sisters. Grant us the grace to forgive as we have been forgiven and help us lean into Your daily provisions, trusting that You are our ultimate provider. Amen.

Dive Deeper Daily:

Day 1:

Scripture: Matthew 6:9-13

Focus: The Lord's Prayer as a blueprint for our conversations with God.

Reflection: How often do you refer to the Lord's Prayer in your daily life? Do you see it simply as a recitation, or as a model for deep, intentional conversation with God?

Study Question: Why did Jesus feel the need to teach His disciples a model prayer?

Day 2:

Scripture: Matthew 6:11

Focus: "Give us this day our daily bread."

Reflection: Reflect on your understanding of God as your provider. How do you feel about relying on Him for your daily needs, both physically and spiritually?

Study Question: What is the significance of the word "us" in the prayer? How does it shift your perspective on prayer?

Day 3:

Scripture: Numbers 11:9

Focus: God's provision of manna in the wilderness.

Reflection: Recall a time when you experienced God's provision in an unexpected way. How did that experience shape your understanding of God?

Study Question: How does the story of manna in the wilderness parallel Jesus's teaching in the Lord's Prayer?

Day 4:

Scripture: John 6:35

Focus: Jesus as the Bread of Life.

Reflection: Jesus not only provides for our physical needs but also our spiritual hunger. How do you feed your spiritual hunger daily?

Study Question: Why is it important to understand Jesus as the Bread of Life when reflecting on our daily needs?

Day 5:

Scripture: Matthew 6:31-34

Focus: Seek first the Kingdom of God.

Reflection: What are the worries that dominate your thoughts? How can focusing on God's kingdom and righteousness shift your perspective?

Study Question: How does seeking God's kingdom relate to trusting Him for our daily needs?

Day 6:

Scripture: Matthew 6:12

Focus: The intertwining of daily provision and daily forgiveness.

Reflection: Reflect on the balance between acknowledging our daily physical needs and our spiritual need for forgiveness. How do you prioritize these in your prayers?

Study Question: Why did Jesus link our need for bread (provision) and forgiveness?

Day 7:

Scripture: Luke 6:27-28; Matthew 5:23-24

Focus: The call to forgive others.

Reflection: Reflect on any unforgiveness in your heart. What steps can you take today to release this burden and embrace the freedom of forgiveness?

Study Question: Why does Jesus place such a strong emphasis on forgiving others as a part of our relationship with God?

Closing Thought: As we approach God in prayer, let us remember that it is not just about our individual needs. We are called to pray for and with one another, recognizing our shared humanity and the grace we all need from God daily.

CHAPTER 10

Devotional: Relying on God in Temptation

Scripture Reading: Matthew 6:9-13

Reflection: The Lord's Prayer, as depicted in Matthew 6:9-13, is more than just a model prayer; it's an intimate conversation with God. This prayer encapsulates our need for daily provision, forgiveness, and most crucially, protection against temptation and evil.

We are constantly exposed to temptations in our daily lives. These trials are not designed to showcase our weaknesses but to test our strengths. However, we're not alone. God's protective shield is always around us. We need to remember that while God doesn't tempt us, He does allow temptations to occur. In these moments, He also provides a way out for us.

When faced with temptation, it's essential to remember that Satan knows our weaknesses. However, our strength comes from relying on God's protection and guidance. Just as the neighbor's dog was contained by an invisible fence, God sets boundaries around us to protect us from harm.

Study Questions:

1. **Understanding the Scripture:** Why is the Lord's Prayer referred to as the Model Prayer?

2. **Reflecting on Your Life:** In what areas of your life do you feel you're most vulnerable to temptation?

3. **Digging Deeper:** How does understanding the difference between a test and a temptation change your perspective on challenges?

4. **Personal Reflection:** How does the image of God as a protective fence resonate with your own experiences?

5. **Practical Application:** How can you actively seek God's guidance and protection in your daily life?

6. **Relevance:** Why is it significant to understand that while God allows temptation, He doesn't lead us into it?

Prayer: Dear Heavenly Father, thank you for your daily provision, forgiveness, and protection. As we face temptations and trials, help us remember that we're not alone. Strengthen us to lean on You and trust Your protective boundaries. Guide us in our daily walk, and let us always remember the hope and promise that You never give us more than we can handle. In Jesus' name, Amen.

Dive Deeper Daily:

Scripture Reading: Matthew 6:9-13

Reflection: Today's scripture offers an intimate look into how Jesus encouraged His followers to communicate with the Father. Recognized as the Lord's Prayer, it provides a framework that covers praise, submission, request, and protection. It underlines the need for God's daily sustenance, forgiveness, and safety.

Key Point: In the given sermon, the preacher emphasizes the interconnectedness of daily sustenance and daily forgiveness, as highlighted by the conjunction "AND" in verse 12. Just as we need our daily bread, we also require the Lord's pardon. More than that, we are reminded that God doesn't lead us into temptation; instead, He allows it. But He provides a way out, illustrating His protective nature.

Today's Prayer: "Father in Heaven, I approach Your throne with humility. I recognize Your sovereignty and thank You for Your daily provisions. Please forgive my shortcomings as I strive to forgive those who've wronged me. Guide me away from temptations and protect me from evil. I put my trust in You, knowing You won't let any trial be more than I can handle. In Jesus' name, Amen."

Study Questions:

1. Why is the Lord's Prayer often referred to as the "Model Prayer"? How can you use it as a blueprint in your prayer life?

2. Reflect on the 'thy-petitions' and 'us-petitions.' What do they reveal about our relationship with God and our needs?

61

3. The sermon discusses the conjunction "AND" as being significant. How does this word connect our need for daily bread and daily forgiveness?

4. The sermon distinguishes between a test from God and a temptation not from God. How can this understanding shape your perception of challenges you face in life?

5. The preacher used the analogy of the 'feisty dog' to describe God's protection over us from evil. How does this analogy resonate with you in your spiritual journey?

6. According to 1 Corinthians 10:13, God provides a way out of temptation. Can you recall a time when you witnessed God making a way of escape for you?

Challenge for the Day: Today, consciously take note of moments when you feel tempted or tested. In those moments, remember the Lord's Prayer and reflect on God's guidance and protection. Remember, He has built a fence around you, and His protection is real.

Let this devotional inspire you to engage more deeply in your prayer life, recognizing God's provision, pardon, and protection. No matter what challenges you face, remember there is always hope with God.

CHAPTER 11

Devotional: Finding Hope at the Intersection of Pain and Promise

Scripture Reading: Matthew 6:9-13

Reflection: Scripture today reminds us of the vastness of God's love and mercy. In our journey through life, we often find ourselves walking down the street of pain, struggle, and despair. It feels like the weight of the world is on our shoulders, and our hope is waning. But just like the widow from Nain, when we reach our lowest point, that's when we find Jesus, standing at the intersection of our pain and His promise.

Jesus understands our pain. He recognizes our sorrow. And in our darkest moments, He offers us His promise – a promise of hope, restoration, and new life. Through His compassion, our pain gives way to His promise, which further leads us to our purpose. It's a transformational journey from despair to joy, from hopelessness to purpose-filled living.

God has a plan for each one of us. Even in the bleakest moments, when we think all is lost, He is orchestrating events for our good. It's a journey from pain, through His promise, discovering our purpose, and recognizing His grand plan.

The widow's son was restored to life, a symbolism of God's redeeming love bringing us from death to life. The city of Nain, meaning "Green Pastures," serves as a reminder that God wants to lead us to places of rest, restoration, and revival. He desires to turn our mourning into dancing and our sorrow into joy.

Remember, at the intersection of Pain St. and Promise Rd., Jesus is waiting, ready to turn your life around. So, cling to His promises, embrace His purpose for you, and trust in His plan. In Him, pain transforms into power, and despair becomes a testimony of hope.

Study Questions:

1. **Personal Reflection**: Can you recall a time in your life when you felt like you were descending from the top of a hill down to a valley of despair? How did God show up for you at that moment?

2. In the sermon, two crowds are mentioned: one following the widow (representing pain) and the other following Jesus (representing promise). **Discussion**: What does it mean for you to transition from the crowd of pain to the crowd of promise?

3. The widow's pain was evident, but Jesus' promise was even more profound. **Reflection**: How can you lean into God's promises when experiencing personal pain or watching others suffer?

4. **Meditation on Scripture**: Read Jeremiah 29:11. What does this verse mean to you in the context of your current life circumstances?

5. **Practical Application**: How can you actively turn from Pain St. onto Promise Rd. in your daily life? What steps can you take to align more closely with God's purpose and plan for you?

6. The city of Nain, meaning "Green Pastures," signifies rest and restoration. **Discussion**: How can you find your "green pasture" in the midst of life's challenges?

7. **Heart Check**: The widow faced a profound loss, yet Jesus intervened with compassion and power. How does Jesus' intervention in the widow's situation reflect His intervention in our lives?

Remember, studying God's Word isn't just about gaining knowledge, but about deepening your relationship with Him. Let the lessons from Luke 7:11-15 comfort, guide, and inspire you on your journey with Christ.

Dive Deeper Daily:

Day 1 - Recognizing the Pain

Scripture Reading: Luke 7:11-12

Reflection: In our lives, we face various forms of pain and adversity. Some days we feel on top of the world, and other times, we're plummeting to the depths of despair. Consider a time when you felt like everything was going wrong. What brought you to that point?

Study Question: Why do you think the author emphasized the positioning of Nain being on a hill, but its gate being at the bottom?

Day 2 - Compassionate Intersection

Scripture Reading: Luke 7:13

Reflection: At our lowest points, Jesus meets us with compassion and hope. The intersection of our pain with God's promises can be transformational. Have you ever experienced such an intersection? How did it feel?

Study Question: What does Jesus' instruction to "weep not" signify?

Day 3 - Promise of Resurrection

Scripture Reading: Luke 7:14-15

Reflection: God has a unique way of turning our pain into purpose. Just when we think a situation is beyond hope, He can bring about resurrection and new life. Where in your life do you need a touch from Jesus today?

Study Question: How does Jesus' action in these verses demonstrate His power over life and death?

Day 4 - God's Plan Amid Pain

Scripture Reading: Jeremiah 29:11

Reflection: God's promises are firm. Even when we can't see the path forward, He has a plan and purpose for us. How does knowing God's promises provide comfort during challenging times?

Study Question: What does Jeremiah 29:11 reveal about God's intentions for us?

Day 5 - Peace Beyond Understanding

Scripture Reading: Philippians 4:7

Reflection: After every storm comes a sense of calm. God's peace surpasses all understanding and anchors us, even when the waves of life threaten to overwhelm. How have you experienced God's peace?

Study Question: How can you actively seek God's peace in your daily life?

Day 6 - Green Pastures

Scripture Reading: Psalm 23:1-3

Reflection: Just as Nain means "Green Pastures," God promises to lead us to places of rest and rejuvenation. How can you find your own "green pasture" in today's world?

Study Question: What does the imagery of "green pastures" represent in our relationship with God?

Day 7 - His Everlasting Power

Scripture Reading: Psalm 23:4-6

Reflection: Through every valley and shadow, God is with us, providing comfort and guidance. His power turns pain into promise, purpose, and plan. Reflect on a time when you felt God's power guiding you out of a challenging situation.

Study Question: How does Psalm 23 encapsulate the journey from Pain St. to Promise Rd.?

Conclusion: As you reflect on this week's devotional, remember that no matter the pains and challenges you face, God is ready to intersect with your journey, turning your path from despair to hope, from pain to promise. Embrace His plans, promises, and the peace He offers, knowing that His power will always guide you.

CHAPTER 12

Devotional: Healing the Wounds of Hypocrisy

Scripture Reading: Matthew 23:25-28

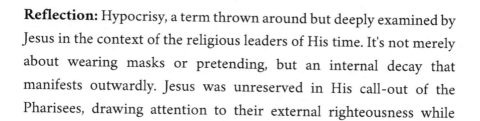

Reflection: Hypocrisy, a term thrown around but deeply examined by Jesus in the context of the religious leaders of His time. It's not merely about wearing masks or pretending, but an internal decay that manifests outwardly. Jesus was unreserved in His call-out of the Pharisees, drawing attention to their external righteousness while their hearts were far from Him.

But instead of just pointing fingers, let's introspect. Are there areas in our lives where we too are living a facade? Places where our beliefs and our actions are not aligned? As believers, our ultimate goal should be to reflect Christ in every facet of our life. Yet, when we fall into the trap of hypocrisy, not only do we drift away from Christ, but we also inadvertently push others away. It's time for self-examination and repentance, allowing God to cleanse us from the inside out.

Personal Application: Are you living a life of authenticity in Christ? Or are there parts of your life where you feel you're putting on a mask, not living up to what you preach or believe?

Prayer: Lord, search our hearts and show us areas of hypocrisy. Help us to live lives that are genuine and authentic, reflecting Your love and truth in all we do. Amen.

Study Questions:

1. **Reflection on Personal Experiences:** Can you recall a time when you witnessed hypocrisy in the church or in your own life? How did it make you feel? How did it affect your relationship with God and others?

2. **Examining the Heart:** Matthew 23:25-28 talks about the internal state being of utmost importance. Why is it so crucial for our internal selves to be aligned with God before we can effectively minister or show Christ to others?

3. **Bridging Understanding:** Why do you think hypocrisy is so damaging, especially within the church setting?

4. **The Role of Repentance:** Mark 1:15 emphasizes repentance. How does repentance play a role in addressing and healing from hypocrisy?

5. **Walking in Authenticity:** Based on this sermon, what are some practical steps believers can take to guard against hypocrisy in their personal lives and in their communities?

Use these study questions as a guide for your personal or group reflection on the topic of hypocrisy in the church and how we can strive for authenticity in our walk with Christ.

Dive Deeper Daily:

Day 1: Recognizing Hypocrisy Within

Scripture Reading: Matthew 23:25-28

Reflection: Have you ever witnessed or been part of hypocrisy? How does it feel to be on either side? Reflect on Jesus' words against hypocrisy in today's verses.

Prayer: Lord, expose the areas of hypocrisy in my life, so I may walk in truth and integrity.

Day 2: The Standards We Set

Scripture Reading: Matthew 7:3-5

Reflection: Do you hold others to a higher standard than you do yourself? How can you avoid being judgmental?

Prayer: Father, give me a heart that is quick to extend grace and slow to judge. Let me see others through your eyes.

Day 3: Reflecting Christ's Love

Scripture Reading: Matthew 15:8

Reflection: Are your words in alignment with your heart? How can you ensure your actions and words reflect the love of Christ?

Prayer: Jesus, let my heart draw close to You. May my words and actions be a true reflection of Your love.

Day 4: Focusing on the Inside

Scripture Reading: Matthew 23:26

Reflection: How often do you focus on outward appearances rather than the condition of your heart? What changes can you make to prioritize inner transformation?

Prayer: Lord, cleanse my heart and renew a right spirit within me. Let my outward actions be a reflection of my inward faith.

Day 5: Holding True to God's Word

Scripture Reading: Revelation 3:16

Reflection: How can you avoid being lukewarm in your faith? In what ways can you hold onto the truth of God's word without compromise?

Prayer: Holy Spirit, keep my heart fervent for You. Let me be zealous in my pursuit of truth and righteousness.

Study Questions:

1. In Matthew 23, Jesus strongly rebukes the Pharisees for their hypocrisy. Why do you think hypocrisy was such a significant issue for Him?

2. The sermon points out the dangers of holding others to a higher standard than oneself. How can this lead to hurt and damage in a church community?

3. Reflect on the illustration of the Infiniti Q45. In what ways do we sometimes prioritize outward appearances over genuine integrity?

4. Discuss the implications of the Prosperity Gospel as mentioned in the sermon. How can a skewed understanding of prosperity lead to disillusionment and pain?

5. Jesus warns about those who prophesy in His name but whom He does not know. How can we ensure our relationship with Jesus is genuine and not just based on outward religious practices?

6. How can the church combat hypocrisy and work towards creating an environment of genuine love, acceptance, and growth?

May this devotional guide you through a week of reflection, drawing closer to God and understanding the depth of His word and love.

CHAPTER 13

Devotional: Taming the Tongue

Scripture Reading: James 1:26, Ephesians 4:29

Reflection: Gossip, though seemingly harmless, is like a spark that can ignite a vast forest fire. It can destroy relationships, reputations, and spiritual growth. The Bible is clear about the dangers of the tongue and the damage it can cause when not used wisely.

James 1:26 reminds us that just appearing religious isn't enough. If we don't control our tongues, we deceive ourselves and our religious practices become meaningless. It's a poignant reminder that our actions must mirror our beliefs.

Ephesians 4:29 further emphasizes this by cautioning against unwholesome talk. Instead, our words should uplift and benefit others. This guideline is clear, but many still struggle with keeping their words in check.

Why does gossip seem so enticing? Why do we feel the urge to share something juicy even when we know it's potentially harmful? Our own nature and society play a role, but it's also our responsibility to resist the temptation.

Taming the tongue isn't just about avoiding gossip. It's about choosing words that heal, inspire, and uplift. It's about bridging gaps and creating bonds of trust. The question we must ask ourselves is, "Am I building up or tearing down?"

Reflection Questions:

1. **Personal Evaluation:** Can you recall a recent instance where you engaged in gossip or unwholesome talk? How did it make you feel afterward?

2. **Purposeful Speech:** Ephesians 4:29 tells us to only speak what is beneficial for others. How can you apply this principle in your daily conversations?

3. **The THINK Rule:** Before speaking, consider if what you're about to say is True, Helpful, Inspiring, Necessary, and Kind. How might this rule help you in your interactions?

4. **Impact on Spiritual Growth:** Reflect on the idea that gossip and uncontrolled speech can hinder spiritual growth. Why do you think this is the case, and how can you ensure that your words lead to growth rather than stagnation?

5. **Responding to Gossip:** If someone starts gossiping to you, consider the strategies provided: asking why they're telling you, suggesting ways to help the person, and asking if they've prayed for them. How might these strategies change the course of the conversation?

Prayer: Heavenly Father, help me to guard my tongue and use my words wisely. Let my words be a reflection of Your love and grace. Teach me to speak in ways that uplift and benefit others. Help me resist the temptation of gossip and unwholesome talk. May the words of my mouth and the meditation of my heart always be pleasing to You. Amen.

Dive Deeper Daily:

Scripture Reading: James 1:26 & Ephesians 4:29

Devotional: Gossip is a silent weapon that has the power to destroy trust, reputations, and relationships. Even if unintentional, its aftermath is damaging. Every time we are tempted to share or entertain information that is not beneficial or edifying, let us remember that God calls us to a higher standard. He wants our words to heal, uplift, and bring life. The words we speak hold power, and they reflect the condition of our heart and the depth of our relationship with Christ. Let's challenge ourselves today to choose our words carefully and to be a beacon of grace and love.

Study Questions:

1. What does the Bible say about the consequences of not controlling one's tongue?

2. How does the poem "My name is Gossip" relate to your personal experiences or observations?

3. What is the difference between gossip and speaking the truth?

4. How does the acronym T.H.I.N.K. help us control our speech? Can you think of a situation where you could apply this acronym before speaking?

5. Proverbs 18:8 suggests that gossip can be alluring, almost like "choice morsels". Why do you think people find gossip so enticing?

6. How can engaging in gossip indirectly harm one's spiritual relationship with God?

7. Why do you think God places so much importance on the words we speak?

8. Reflecting on Proverbs 17:4, have you ever found yourself being more attentive to negative or gossipy conversations? Why do you think that is?

9. How can we respond or change the topic when someone starts to gossip in our presence?

10. Psalm 15:1-3 describes the characteristics of someone who dwells with the Lord. Reflect on these verses. What areas of your speech life need refining to align with this standard?

Reflection & Prayer: Father, I confess that there are times I have indulged in gossip or have not controlled my tongue as I should. Help me to understand the power and impact of my words. May I always strive to speak words that uplift, heal, and edify others, honoring you in all I say and do. Amen.

CHAPTER 14

Devotional: Same Water, Different Boat

Scripture Reading: James 1:26; Ephesians 4:29; John 8; John 7:24; 1 Corinthians 5:12; Romans 14:9-10; Matthew 7:2; 1 Corinthians 4:5; Galatians 6:2

Reflection: Judgment has a power unlike any other. It divides and pushes away. It sows seeds of discord and pain. When we judge, we fail to reflect Christ's love, and we cause harm to those who are searching for God's grace.

Jesus was our greatest example of love and compassion. He encountered the woman caught in adultery, whom the crowd was eager to stone. But instead of condemning her, Jesus stooped low and defended her, urging those without sin to cast the first stone. This story is a stark reminder of our own sinfulness and the need for God's grace.

Each one of us is in a boat. Some boats are large, some small. Some are new, some old. But we all float on the same water, under the watchful eyes of the same God. Before we judge, let's remember that we all have holes in our boats, and only by God's grace do we continue to float.

Judgment creates an atmosphere of hostility, but love fosters healing and reconciliation. Let us strive to be a reflection of Jesus, seeking to build up rather than tear down.

Study Questions:

1. **Self-reflection**: Have you ever been judged or felt the hurt from someone's judgment? How did it feel?

2. What does James 1:26 teach about the importance of bridling our tongues?

3. In the story of the woman caught in adultery (John 8), what can we learn about Jesus' response to sin and how He treats those who are judged by others?

4. How does the "Same Water, Different Boat" illustration help us understand our place in relation to others and God?

5. Why do you think people feel the need to judge others? What does this reveal about their own insecurities or shortcomings?

6. Romans 14:10 reminds us that we will all stand before the judgment seat of Christ. How does this knowledge shape how you interact with others?

7. Reflect on 1 Corinthians 4:5. Why is it essential not to judge others prematurely?

8. How can we practice accountability with one another without descending into judgment?

9. What steps can you take to ensure that you do not become a stumbling block to someone else's journey to Christ?

10. Reflect on the water bottle illustration from the sermon. How does it resonate with your understanding of value and worth in Christ?

Prayer: Lord Jesus, forgive us for the times we have judged others, forgetting our own need for Your grace. Help us to be a reflection of Your love and compassion, building up and encouraging those around us. May our lives and our words draw others closer to You. In Your name, we pray. Amen.

Dive Deeper Daily:

Reflection Scripture: James 1:26, Ephesians 4:29

Devotional: Today, let's take a moment to reflect on the powerful message from the sermon, "Same Water, Different Boat." As believers, it's easy to become so focused on our personal relationship with Christ that we unintentionally become judgmental towards others. We forget that we were all once in a state of sin and that Christ saved us with His unconditional love.

Remember that judgment causes rifts – between friends, families, believers, and non-believers. The weight of judgment has led many away from the church. Let us challenge ourselves to be bearers of love, grace, and mercy, just as Jesus has been to us. We are all on a spiritual journey, floating on the same water. Our boats might look different, but the water remains the same.

Study Questions:

1. **Self-Reflection:** In what areas of your life do you find yourself being most judgmental? Why do you think that is?

2. **Scriptural Context:** Read the account of the woman caught in adultery in John 8. Why do you think Jesus responded the way He did? What can we learn from His reaction?

3. **Comparative Analysis:** How do James 1:26 and Ephesians 4:29 provide guidance in our daily interactions? Why is it essential to "keep a tight rein" on our tongue?

4. **Personal Application:** Considering the "Same Water, Different Boat" analogy, in what ways have you perhaps unfairly judged someone because their "boat" looked different from yours? How can you amend this behavior?

5. **Heart Check:** The story shared about the value of a water bottle in various places was powerful. How do you value others based on their current "place" or circumstances? How can you remind yourself of the intrinsic value of every person in God's eyes?

6. **Encouragement:** Think of someone who might feel judged or isolated from the church or community. What steps can you take this week to show them love and acceptance?

Prayer: Heavenly Father, thank You for reminding us that we are all on a spiritual journey. Help us to refrain from being judgmental and instead be bearers of Your love, grace, and mercy. As we sail on this vast ocean of life, let our hearts be aligned with Yours, seeing every soul as invaluable. In Jesus' name, we pray. Amen.

CHAPTER 15

Devotional: Shifting from Division to Unity

Scripture Reading: 1 Corinthians 1:10

"Now I beseech you, brethren, by the name of our Lord Jesus Christ, that ye all speak the same thing, and that there be no divisions among you; but that ye be perfectly joined together in the same mind and in the same judgment."

Reflection: In the world we live in, division is rampant. Whether it's politics, social issues, or even personal relationships, division seems to be the norm. As believers, though, we're called to a different standard. God calls us to unity.

The Apostle Paul passionately implored the Corinthians to seek unity. Not a false unity built on compromise, but a genuine unity founded on Christ's love. This unity doesn't mean we're all the same; rather, it means we have the same goal, the same purpose. Just as every player in a football team has a unique role but works towards a common aim, we too, in the body of Christ, each have a role to play. Yet, our purpose remains singular: to glorify Christ.

However, unity can easily be broken by personal ambitions, pride, and misunderstandings. When our focus shifts from Jesus to ourselves, divisions arise. But, Paul reminds us that these divisions aren't insurmountable. Through the power of Christ and the guidance of the Holy Spirit, we can bridge these divides and restore unity.

Today, let's commit to fostering unity in our churches, families, and communities. Let's pray for God's guidance to help us see past our differences and to work together for His glory.

Reflection Questions:

1. **Personal Reflection:** In what areas of your life have you witnessed division? How can you be an instrument of peace and unity in those situations?

2. **In Depth:** Paul used the word "schisma" (translated as divisions), which indicates a tear but not a complete break. Can you think of a situation where division felt like a tear, but there was hope for restoration? How did you address it?

3. **Practical Application:** What are some practical ways you can promote unity in your church or community? How can you actively seek reconciliation where division exists?

4. **Scriptural Insight:** In Matthew 18:15-16, Jesus provided guidance on addressing grievances among believers. How can we apply this teaching in our interactions with fellow Christians?

5. **Worldly Vs. Heavenly Perspective:** Dr. Martin Luther King, Jr. highlighted the division even within the church with regards to race. How can we, as the body of Christ, set an example of unity for the world to see?

6. **Heart Check:** Reflect on the fruits of the Spirit (Galatians 5:22-23). How can these qualities assist in mending divisions and fostering unity?

7. **Future Vision:** How will striving for unity now impact the future of the church, its mission, and its testimony to the world?

As we reflect on the sermon and dive deeper into the essence of unity, let us remember the words of Psalm 133:1, "Behold, how good and how pleasant it is for brethren to dwell together in unity!" Let unity in Christ be our aim, and may we work tirelessly to uphold it.

Dive Deeper Daily:

Verse of the Day: *"Now I beseech you, brethren, by the name of our Lord Jesus Christ, that ye all speak the same thing, and that there be no divisions among you; but that ye be perfectly joined together in the same mind and in the same judgment."* - 1 Corinthians 1:10

Reflection: Unity doesn't mean uniformity. It means moving together in harmony, even with our differences, towards the same goal. Just as an orchestra, with different instruments, creates a symphony, we as the body of Christ should come together in our varied roles to create harmony. We are reminded today that we are all part of the body of Christ and, though we have our differences, our unity in purpose and goal is what binds us together.

Study Questions:

1. What stood out to you in the sermon about the distinction between unity and uniformity?

2. Why do you think the Apostle Paul felt such a strong need to address division within the church?

3. What are the dangers and impacts of division, both within a church and in our broader society?

4. How can we apply the biblical principle of unity in our daily lives and in our interactions with others?

5. In what ways can you personally contribute to fostering unity within your community or congregation?

6. Why is it important for believers to remember that their battle is not against flesh and blood, but against spiritual forces?

7. Reflect on 1 Thessalonians 5:11. How can you encourage and build up those around you today?

8. What can the metaphor of the body, as described in 1 Corinthians 12, teach us about the value of every individual within the church?

9. Why is it crucial for believers to maintain unity despite differences in denominations, race, or political views?

10. Reflect on the closing of the sermon with Aesop's fable. How does this story emphasize the importance of unity? In what areas of your life can you apply this lesson?

Prayer: Lord Jesus, teach us the true meaning of unity. Help us to recognize that our strength lies in our collective effort, bound together by Your love. May we always remember that our fight is not against our brothers and sisters, but against the spiritual forces of darkness. Fill us with a spirit of humility and guide us to promote unity in our communities. In Your mighty name, we pray. Amen.

CHAPTER 16

Devotional: "Passing on a Legacy of Faith"

Scripture Reading: Psalm 78

Reflection: Psalm 78 is not just a recounting of the past; it's a guide for the future. Asaph wasn't merely recollecting historical events; he was framing a legacy to ensure that future generations would have strong roots in their faith. Every story he recounted was a testament to God's faithfulness in the face of human failings. By reminding the generations of God's acts, he hoped to encourage trust, faithfulness, and obedience in their hearts.

Through this Psalm, we are reminded of our role today. We too have the responsibility to pass on the stories of God's goodness to the generations after us, to ensure they know Him, trust Him, and walk with Him.

Application: It's not just about knowing the stories but internalizing their meaning. Let's be diligent in sharing God's works with the younger generation, ensuring they understand and hold onto the faith.

Prayer: Lord, thank You for Your acts in the past and for their reminder to us today. Help us be diligent in sharing Your goodness with the next generation. May they grow in faith and knowledge of You, just as we have. Amen.

Study Questions for "Passing on a Legacy of Faith":

1. **Understanding the Author:** Asaph played a significant role during King David's reign. How does understanding his position and duties help us appreciate his perspective in Psalm 78?

2. **Generational Faith:** Why is it important for every generation to pass on their experiences and understanding of God to the next?

3. **God's Deeds:** Asaph chose to highlight specific acts of God in this Psalm. Which acts of God stood out to you the most and why?

4. **The Power of Stories:** Asaph used stories of God's deeds to teach lessons about Him. Why are stories a powerful medium to convey truths about God?

5. **Forgetting God:** Asaph pointed out that people often forgot God's deeds, leading them into trouble. What practical steps can we take to ensure we don't forget God's acts in our lives?

6. **Applying the Teaching:** The Psalm is labeled as a "Maskil" which means a teaching. How can we take the lessons from this Psalm and teach them to our children or the younger generation around us?

7. **Personal Reflection:** Think of a time when you experienced God's faithfulness. How can you share that story with someone else, especially someone younger, to encourage their faith?

Use these questions to dive deeper into the sermon and understand the importance of passing on faith and remembering God's deeds.

Dive Deeper Daily:

Day 1:

Scripture Reading: Psalm 78:1-4

Devotional Thought: Asaph recognized the importance of teaching the next generation about God's wonders and acts. We too have a mandate to pass our faith down, ensuring that it does not become extinct but thrives in future generations.

Reflection Questions:

1. How have you personally experienced God's "wondrous works" in your life?

2. In what ways are you currently passing on your faith to the next generation? If you aren't, what steps can you take to start?

Day 2:

Scripture Reading: Psalm 78:5-7

Devotional Thought: God established His teachings so that each generation might come to know Him, put their confidence in Him, and obey His commands. Our faith story has the power to strengthen the faith of those who come after us.

Reflection Questions:

1. Which stories of faith from your ancestors or church community have impacted your own spiritual journey?

2. How can you ensure that your children or younger believers in your life know about God's deeds?

Day 3:

Scripture Reading: Psalm 78:13-16

Devotional Thought: God is our Deliverer, Guide, and Provider. Whether parting seas, guiding with a fiery light, or providing water from rocks, God's power and provision are evident throughout history.

Reflection Questions:

1. How have you experienced God's guidance, provision, or deliverance in your life?

2. Are there ways in which you're currently in need of God's guidance or provision? How can you lean into His faithfulness in these areas?

Day 4:

Scripture Reading: Psalm 78:32-39

Devotional Thought: Even when the Israelites were unfaithful, God remained compassionate and faithful. He's a forgiving God, understanding our human nature, yet calling us to faithfulness.

Reflection Questions:

1. How does it feel knowing that God remains compassionate and faithful, even when you mess up?

2. Are there areas in your life where you've been unfaithful to God? Take a moment to seek His forgiveness and commit to walking faithfully with Him.

Day 5:

Scripture Reading: Psalm 78:41-43

Devotional Thought: Remembering God's past deeds empowers us to live by faith and not by sight. Forgetting them can lead to a life of unfaithfulness and distance from God.

Reflection Questions:

1. Why is it essential to remember and retell the stories of God's power and redemption?

2. What practices can you incorporate into your daily life to consistently remember God's deeds?

Closing Prayer for the Week:

Lord, like Asaph, may we be ever mindful of the importance of passing our faith onto the next generation. Help us to daily remember and celebrate your faithfulness and to share those stories with those around us. May our lives be a testament to Your unwavering love and power. Amen.

CHAPTER 17

Devotional: When They Go Out of Their Way to Start

Scripture Reading: 1 Samuel 17:1-11

Reflection: David and Goliath, a tale often recounted for its victory. But what's often missed is the journey leading to that moment of triumph. Just like David, we too face Goliaths in our life, towering fears and challenges that seem insurmountable. Our battles might not be with a nine-foot giant, but they are battles of the mind and spirit. Battles with doubt, intimidation, condemnation, and fear. The enemy's tactics may differ, but his goal remains consistent: to divert our focus from God.

The story urges us to remember that our eyes might see the intimidating stature of our problems, and our hearts might waver in doubt, but our spirit, when aligned with God, remains undefeated. The real battle isn't what stands before us but who stands within us.

Meditation: Reflect on a time you faced an intimidating situation. How did you feel? How did you respond? Did you face it on your own or rely on God's strength?

Prayer: Lord, thank you for the reminder that with You on our side, no enemy, no challenge, no Goliath is too great. Help us to always trust in Your power and strength rather than our own. May we always remember that the victory is Yours. Amen.

Study Questions:

1. **Understanding Context**:

   - Describe the scene set in 1 Samuel 17:1-11. Why do you think the Israelites were intimidated by Goliath?

2. **Intimidation**:

   - The sermon points out how Goliath's appearance was used as a tool of intimidation. Can you recall a time in your life where something's appearance or surface-level information made a situation seem more daunting than it actually was?

3. **Doubt**:

   - Goliath planted seeds of doubt among the Israelites. How does doubt hinder our faith walk? Can you think of a Bible character, apart from Eve, who faced doubt? How did they overcome it?

4. **Condemnation**:

   - Goliath tried to belittle the Israelites by comparing them to mere servants of Saul. How does the enemy use condemnation in our lives? What scriptures can we use to combat these condemning thoughts?

5. **Fear**:

- Fear keeps us from stepping out in faith. Reflect on Peter's story. What do you think gave him the confidence to step out of the boat?

6. **Voice of Trust**:

- The sermon highlights the importance of recognizing and trusting God's voice. How can we better attune our ears to hear God's voice amidst the noise of the world?

7. **Personal Reflection**:

- Think of a personal "Goliath" you're currently facing or have faced in the past. How did or can you apply the teachings from this sermon to that situation?

8. **Moving Forward**:

- As believers, how can we prepare ourselves daily so that we are not easily swayed by the enemy's tactics of intimidation, doubt, condemnation, and fear?

Remember, as you delve into these questions and reflect upon them, let the Word of God be your guiding light. The battles we face might be fierce, but the God we serve is fiercer.

Dive Deeper Daily:

Day 1: Setting the Scene

Scripture: 1 Samuel 17:1-3

Reflection: We often look at challenges as if they are insurmountable giants. But before we delve into the story of David and Goliath, consider your personal challenges. How do they seem so much bigger than they are? Remember, giants can be defeated.

Study Question: Why is it important to understand the context and details leading up to a well-known event in the Bible?

Day 2: Seeing the Enemy

Scripture: 1 Samuel 17:4, 1 Peter 5:8

Reflection: Today, we're reminded that what we see isn't always the full story. Goliath may have looked intimidating, but appearances can be deceiving. How have you let appearances or your perceptions deceive you?

Study Question: How does the Bible describe our enemy, the devil?

Day 3: Intimidation Tactics

Scripture: 1 Samuel 17:5-7

Reflection: The enemy uses circumstances to distract us from God. What has been distracting you lately? Are you focused on the size of your problems or the size of your God?

Study Question: What are some other biblical examples where God's people faced intimidating foes or situations?

Day 4: The Weapon of Doubt

Scripture: 1 Samuel 17:8, Genesis 3:1

Reflection: Doubt is a tactic the enemy often uses. It might be a whisper, a question, or a comparison. Recognize when doubt tries to creep into your mind. How will you combat doubt with faith?

Study Question: How did Eve respond to the serpent's question in Genesis, and what can we learn from her response?

Day 5: Fighting the Right Battle

Scripture: Joshua 1:9

Reflection: It's easy to feel like we're in the battle alone, but God reminds us He's always with us. When we face challenges, remember we aren't meant to fight in our own strength.

Study Question: How does relying on God's strength instead of our own change our perspective on challenges?

Day 6: Condemnation vs Conviction

Scripture: 1 Samuel 17:8

Reflection: The enemy tries to condemn us, make us feel unworthy, and mock our faith. But God convicts with love and points us to redemption. How will you differentiate between condemnation and conviction?

Study Question: How did Jesus respond when people tried to condemn others in the New Testament?

Day 7: The Voice of Truth

Scripture: 2 Timothy 1:7

Reflection: Fear is a tool the enemy uses to paralyze us. But God's word reminds us of His love, power, and sound mind. Today, let's drown out the lies of the enemy with the truth of God's Word.

Study Question: In what ways does spending time in God's Word equip us against the tactics of the enemy?

Conclusion:

Reflection: As we end this week, remember to always ask: Whom do you trust? Whom do you serve? Whom do you look to? When giants come, and they will, hold onto the promises of God and step out in faith.

May this week's journey into the lead up to David and Goliath's battle deepen your faith, strengthen your resolve, and help you to stand firm against the tactics of the enemy. Remember, with God on your side, no giant is too big to defeat.

CHAPTER 18

Devotional: Overcoming Family Challenges with the Promise of God

Scripture Reading: 1 Samuel 17:12-29

⸺⸺⸺⸺⸺

Reflection: In our life's journey, there will be obstacles and challenges, some of which will even come from those we hold dearest: our family. It is easy to be disheartened when our very own blood seems to doubt or undermine us. Yet, David's story reminds us that external doubts and challenges do not define our worth or our journey.

David was anointed by God, and though his family and especially his eldest brother questioned his motives and heart, David remained steadfast in his faith and purpose. His confidence wasn't rooted in the acceptance of others, but in the promises of God.

Today's Challenge: In the midst of your trials, will you choose to listen to the naysayers or to God's promises? Will you focus on your earthly reality or God's divine purpose for your life?

Prayer: Lord, help me to focus on Your promises and not on the doubts and criticisms of others. Like David, may my faith be bigger than my fears, and may I always remember the purpose and calling You have placed on my life. In Jesus' name. Amen.

Study Questions:

1. **Reflection on Family Relationships:** David's brother Eliab doubted David's intentions and accused him of being conceited. Have you ever felt misunderstood by your family? How did that affect your relationship with them and with God?

2. **God's Perspective vs. Man's:** 1 Samuel 16:7 reminds us that while man looks at the outward appearance, God looks at the heart. Why do you think people, even family, often judge by external factors? How can we cultivate a heart-focused perspective like God's?

3. **Faith Over Fear:** David faced a tangible giant, but he also had to deal with the "giants" of doubt and criticism. In your life, what "giants" are you facing? How can your faith help you overcome these challenges?

4. **The Power of God's Promises:** The sermon highlighted several scripture verses that emphasize God's promises to us. Choose one of these verses and meditate on it. How does this promise resonate with your current situation?

5. **Taking Action:** David did not let his family's skepticism deter him from his God-given mission. In what ways can you actively choose to trust in God's plan for your life, even when faced with opposition or doubt from those around you?

Use these study questions for personal reflection or to discuss in a small group setting. The story of David and Goliath offers rich insights into navigating challenges with faith, purpose, and resilience.

Dive Deeper Daily:

Day 1

Scripture: 1 Samuel 17:12-14

Reflection: David, the youngest of eight sons, spent his days tending to the family's livestock. Society would often look at the youngest or the seemingly less significant members of the family as having lesser importance. However, God's view differs from human standards. Just like David, you may feel overlooked or undervalued in your family or society. Remember, God doesn't judge by external appearances but looks at the heart.

Study Questions:

1. Have there been times in your life when you felt overlooked or undervalued?

2. How do you think David felt being the youngest and not initially presented before Samuel?

3. How can you remind yourself daily that God sees your heart and values you?

Daily Devotional: Day 2

Scripture: 1 Samuel 16:7

Reflection: God tells Samuel that He doesn't look at outward appearances but rather the heart. In a world filled with comparison and superficial standards, it's easy to feel inadequate. David, although deemed unfit for kingship by human standards, was chosen by God because of his heart. Our worth is not in our physical attributes, achievements, or societal status, but in our heart and relationship with God.

Study Questions:

1. How do you measure your self-worth?

2. How can you cultivate a heart that is pleasing to God?

3. What does it mean to you that God values the heart over outward appearance?

Daily Devotional: Day 3

Scripture: 1 Samuel 17:28

Reflection: Family members can sometimes be the harshest critics. Eliab, David's oldest brother, questions David's motives, belittles him, and accuses him of having a wicked heart. While it might hurt when those closest to us misunderstand or criticize us, we must remember to lean on what God says about us and not let others define our worth.

Study Questions:

1. How would you handle criticism from a close family member or friend?

2. Why do you think Eliab responded to David in such a manner?

3. How can you ensure that your identity is rooted in God's view of you rather than people's opinions?

Daily Devotional: Day 4

Scripture: Psalm 37:23-24

Reflection: Even in our stumbling and shortcomings, God's hand is there to uphold us. David faced numerous challenges, from tending sheep to facing a giant. In every circumstance, his faith and trust in the Lord saw him through. Remember, even when we falter, God's unwavering grip on us remains strong.

Study Questions:

1. Can you recall a time when you stumbled but felt God's hand guiding you through?

2. How does knowing that God upholds you change your perspective on challenges?

3. In what areas of your life do you need to trust that God is holding you firmly?

Daily Devotional: Day 5

Scripture: Isaiah 41:10

Reflection: Fear is an emotion we all grapple with. Whether it's the giants we face daily or the unknowns of the future, God's reassuring word is clear: "Do not fear, for I am with you." David faced Goliath with this unwavering faith. As believers, we have the same God beside us, ready to strengthen and uphold us.

Study Questions:

1. What 'giants' are you currently facing in your life?

2. How does knowing that God is with you provide comfort in fearful situations?

3. How can you cultivate a faith like David's in your daily life?

Feel free to use these devotionals and study questions as a guide for reflection, prayer, and discussion throughout the week.

CHAPTER 19

Devotional: "Strength in Past Victories"

Scripture Reading: 1 Samuel 17:32-40

Reflection: David, the shepherd boy, confronted a challenge that paralyzed an entire army. His secret weapon? The strength of his past victories. Today, we'll dive deep into this truth and explore how our past victories, through God, can empower our present and future. David's willingness to confront Goliath wasn't just youthful exuberance or foolish bravery. It was rooted in a history of God's faithfulness. David remembered the lion and the bear, how God delivered those enemies into his hands. These past victories gave David the assurance that God would do it again.

Similarly, each of us has our own "lions" and "bears" we've faced in the past. Think about those moments. How has God shown up for you before? Maybe it was a financial crisis, health challenges, or emotional storms. If God was faithful then, He will be faithful now.

Consider:

1. Saul's armor did not fit David. It was not only physically cumbersome but was also not a part of David's personal testimony of God's faithfulness. David's sling and stones, on the other hand, were tools he was familiar with and had used under God's guidance before. In our lives, God equips each of us uniquely. The tools, gifts, and experiences He gives us are tailored for the battles we are meant to face. It's essential to embrace what God has given you, rather than comparing or wishing for someone else's armor.

2. David's words remind us that God doesn't need extravagant tools to bring victory. He can use the ordinary to do the extraordinary. Just as Jesus multiplied the five loaves and two fish to feed thousands, God can multiply our small offerings to achieve His purposes.

Prayer: Lord, help me remember the times you've been faithful in my past. Let those memories be my strength today. Equip me with the tools I need for the challenges ahead, and let me embrace them wholeheartedly. Amen.

Study Questions:

1. **Remembering Past Victories:** Can you recall a specific time in your life where God delivered you from a difficult situation? How does that past victory inspire confidence in facing current challenges?

2. **God's Unique Equipping:** Have you ever felt like Saul's armor — trying to use tools or methods that didn't quite fit with how God

made you? How can you identify and utilize the unique tools God has given you?

3. **David's Perspective:** While others saw a giant in Goliath, David saw an opportunity for God to be glorified. How can you shift your perspective to see challenges as opportunities for God to show up?

4. **God's Multiplication:** Like the story of Jesus feeding the 5,000, can you think of a time when God took your small offering and multiplied it for His purposes? How does this encourage you to give your all, no matter how small it might seem?

5. **Stepping out in Faith:** David took a step of faith, trusting in God's past faithfulness. What is one step of faith you can take today, relying on God's history of faithfulness in your life?

Dive Deeper Daily:

Verse of the Day: 1 Samuel 17:37 – "The Lord who rescued me from the paw of the lion and the paw of the bear will rescue me from the hand of this Philistine."

Reflection: David's confidence in God's ability to deliver him from Goliath came not from his own strength or prowess, but from his personal experience of God's faithfulness. David had seen God work in his past, and that gave him confidence for the present. Like David, each of us has a history with God. When we face challenges, we must remember how God has been with us in the past, helping us to move forward in faith.

Study Questions:

1. Why do you think Saul doubted David's ability to fight Goliath? Have you ever faced doubts from others when stepping out in faith?

2. David used the testimonies of his past battles (lion & bear) to strengthen his faith for the current challenge. How can you use your past experiences to build faith for today?

3. What did David mean when he said, "I cannot go with these; for I have not proved them"? How does this apply to our spiritual journey?

4. Why do you think David chose five smooth stones instead of accepting Saul's armor? What does this teach us about relying on God versus relying on human strength or wisdom?

5. David's story encourages us to be available to be used by God. In what areas of your life can you be more available for God's purposes?

Prayer Points:

1. Thank God for the challenges you have overcome with His strength.

2. Pray for faith to trust God in your current situations, remembering how He's acted in your past.

3. Ask God to show you areas where you might be relying more on human strength or wisdom than on Him.

4. Pray for the courage to step out in faith, even when others doubt or discourage you.

5. Ask God to help you be more available for His purposes and plans in your life.

Action Step: Reflect on a time when God helped you overcome a challenge. Write down the details of that experience in a journal. Whenever you face doubts or fears in the future, revisit that entry to remind yourself of God's faithfulness.

CHAPTER 20

Devotional: "Unseen Battles, Unseen Swords"

Scripture Reading: 1 Samuel 17

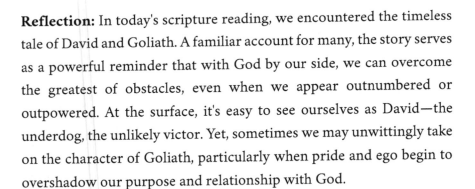

Reflection: In today's scripture reading, we encountered the timeless tale of David and Goliath. A familiar account for many, the story serves as a powerful reminder that with God by our side, we can overcome the greatest of obstacles, even when we appear outnumbered or outpowered. At the surface, it's easy to see ourselves as David—the underdog, the unlikely victor. Yet, sometimes we may unwittingly take on the character of Goliath, particularly when pride and ego begin to overshadow our purpose and relationship with God.

While Goliath saw his strength in physical stature and weapons, David saw his strength in the Lord. It wasn't the stone or the sling that gave David the victory—it was his unwavering faith in God. As the sermon so poignantly highlighted: David showed up, trusted God, and was in the right place to receive his victory. Yet, the sword was absent from his hand.

Sometimes, God will use our battles to equip us with tools and strengths we never knew we needed. David's victory not only defeated the giant but also equipped him with a sword for future battles. Just like David, God may be preparing us through our struggles, granting us unseen swords for unseen battles.

As you reflect on today's message, consider the battles you're facing. Are they molding and equipping you for what's ahead? Are you approaching them with humility and trust in God, or are you leaning on your own strength and understanding?

Study Questions:

1. **Self-Reflection:** In what areas of your life might you be acting like Goliath? Where might you be "too big for your britches"?

2. **Power of Words:** Goliath used his words to intimidate and belittle. How do you use your words daily? Are they uplifting or destructive?

3. **Trust in Possessions:** Like Goliath, we often place too much trust in our possessions or accomplishments. What are you placing your trust in instead of God?

4. **Unseen Battles:** David's victory against Goliath equipped him with a sword for future challenges. What "unseen swords" might God be giving you through your current battles?

5. **Humility:** How can you cultivate a humble spirit in a world that often values pride and self-sufficiency over reliance on God?

6. **Action Step:** Based on today's sermon, what is one tangible step you can take this week to ensure you're approaching life more like David than Goliath?

May this devotional guide you deeper into the message of David and Goliath, prompting self-examination and growth in faith. Remember, it's not the size of the battle, but the size of our God that matters most.

Dive Deeper Daily:

Day 1: Humility in Leadership

Scripture: Romans 12:3 (NIV) - "Do not think of yourself more highly than you ought, but rather think of yourself with sober judgment, in accordance with the faith God has distributed to each of you."

Reflection: In your daily walk, consider the positions of leadership or influence you hold. Reflect on how you perceive and treat others within these roles. Are you leading with humility, or has pride crept into your heart?

Study Questions:

1. In what areas of life might you be tempted to 'get the big head'?

2. How does humility affect your ability to lead or influence others?

Prayer: Heavenly Father, grant me a heart of humility. Help me to see others as You see them and treat them with the love and respect they deserve. Amen.

Day 2: The Power of Words

Scripture: Proverbs 10:19 (NLT) - "Too much talk leads to sin. Be sensible and keep your mouth shut."

Reflection: Words have the power to build up or tear down. Reflect on your speech patterns and the impact they have on those around you. Are your words a source of encouragement or a cause for hurt?

Study Questions:

1. Can you recall a time when your words ran ahead of you, leading to regret?

2. What steps can you take to become more mindful of your speech?

Prayer: Lord, help me to tame my tongue. Let my words be a source of life and not destruction. Guide me to speak only what is helpful for building others up. Amen.

Day 3: The Magnitude of God's Power

Scripture: 1 Samuel 17:36 (NIV) - "Your servant has killed both the lion and the bear; this uncircumcised Philistine will be like one of them, because he has defied the armies of the living God."

Reflection: David's confidence lay not in his own strength but in the might of God. Reflect on your own life challenges. Are you underestimating God's power to see you through?

Study Questions:

1. How can past victories and trials strengthen your faith for present battles?

2. In what areas of your life might you be underestimating God's power?

Prayer: Almighty God, forgive me for the times I've underestimated You. Help me to remember Your past faithfulness as I face current challenges. Strengthen my faith in Your mighty power. Amen.

Day 4: The Futility of Earthly Possessions

Scripture: 1 Samuel 17:45 (NIV) - "David said to the Philistine, 'You come against me with sword and spear and javelin, but I come against you in the name of the Lord Almighty, the God of the armies of Israel, whom you have defied.'"

Reflection: Reflect on the things you rely on for security and success. Are these things taking the place of God in your life?

Study Questions:

1. What possessions or achievements might you be putting too much trust in?

2. How can you shift your reliance from these earthly things to God?

Prayer: Lord, help me to not place my trust in possessions or achievements. Remind me that true security and success come from relying on You. Teach me to trust in Your name above all else. Amen.

Day 5: Victory in Surrender

Scripture: 1 Samuel 17:50 (KJV) - "So David prevailed over the Philistine with a sling and with a stone, and smote the Philistine, and slew him; but there was no sword in the hand of David."

Reflection: David's victory came not from his own armament but from his trust in God. Reflect on the battles you're facing. Are you trying to fight in your own strength or are you surrendering to God?

Study Questions:

1. How does surrendering to God lead to victory in your battles?

2. What is the significance of David not having a sword in his hand during his victory?

Prayer: Heavenly Father, I surrender my battles to You. Help me to trust in Your strength and not my own. I praise You for the victory that comes from relying on You alone. Amen.

CHAPTER 21

Devotional: The Life-Giving Breath of Encouragement

Scripture Reading: Romans 1:12

Reflection: Encouragement isn't just a pat on the back or a fleeting compliment. It is the very breath of God that gives life to drooping spirits, renews hope in distressed hearts, and kindles passion in weary souls. Encouragement is God's design for us to help one another stand strong in faith, and to remind us of our identity and worth in Him.

Just as Moses found strength in God's encouragement, we too can draw strength from the support and encouragement of our brothers and sisters in Christ. It's a beautiful cycle: as we receive encouragement, we are emboldened to offer it to others. And as we offer it, we create a ripple effect, impacting the lives of countless individuals, fostering unity and building a vibrant, loving community of believers.

Today, may we recognize the divine power of encouragement. Let us make it our mission to breathe life, hope, and inspiration into the hearts of those around us. In doing so, we reflect God's love, play our part in building His kingdom, and experience the joy of true fellowship.

Study Questions:

1. **Reflection on Personal Experience:** Can you recall a time when someone's encouragement significantly impacted your faith or decisions? How did it make you feel, and what did you learn about the power of encouragement from that experience?

2. **Diving Deeper:** Moses received encouragement directly from God. In today's world, how can we ensure that our encouragement to others is rooted in God's Word and His promises?

3. **Applying the Word:** 1 Thessalonians 5:11 urges us to encourage one another and build each other up. How can you practically implement this directive in your daily life?

4. **The Impact of Encouragement:** How does encouragement differ from mere compliments? Why is it important to encourage with sincerity and truth?

5. **Unity in the Body:** How can encouragement lead to unity within the church community? What are some barriers to encouragement in our communities, and how can we overcome them?

6. **Stepping Out:** The sermon mentioned encouragement inspiring us to step out of our comfort zones. How can you step out in faith this week, encouraged by God's promises and the support of your community?

7. **Prayerful Reflection:** Spend some time in prayer, asking God to place someone on your heart who needs encouragement. Ask for the words, actions, or gestures that would best lift that person's spirit.

As you ponder these questions and reflect on the sermon, may you be inspired to become a beacon of encouragement in your community, drawing from the inexhaustible well of God's love and grace.

Dive Deeper Daily:

"When we get together, I want to encourage you in your faith, but I also want to be encouraged by yours." - Romans 1:12 (NLT)

Encouragement is like oxygen to the soul. More than just words, it's the infusion of hope, strength, and worth. Today, as we navigate through life's intricacies, let us remember the power of encouragement. It doesn't merely change a mood; it changes destinies. Encouragement is God's instrument in our hands, a reflection of His heart, and a demonstration of His love.

When you face challenges today, remember Moses. Amidst the grumbling of the Israelites and the pressures of leadership, it was God's encouragement that upheld him. Similarly, God's encouragement for us is ever-present, waiting to be discovered in His Word, in our prayers, and through our community.

Today, let's not underestimate the transformative power of an encouraging word or deed. In a divided world, our encouragement can be a bridge, uniting the hearts and forging bonds in the body of Christ.

Let your words and actions today reflect God's heart, and watch as they breathe life into those around you.

Study Questions for Reflection:

1. **The Source of Encouragement:** How do you perceive encouragement differently after understanding its spiritual power as described in the sermon? How does God's role in encouragement shape our responsibility?

2. **Historical Reflection:** How did encouragement impact Moses' journey with the Israelites? Can you think of other biblical figures who were significantly influenced by encouragement?

3. **The Hope in Encouragement:** Reflect on a time when a word of encouragement acted as a balm for your soul. How did it help reshape your perspective during that difficult time?

4. **Inspiration to Act:** Recall an instance when encouragement inspired you to take a step of faith. How did it alter your trajectory or deepen your relationship with God?

5. **The Role in Unity:** How does encouragement play a role in fostering unity within the body of Christ? Why is this particularly crucial in our current global context?

6. **Being an Encourager:** Considering the deep impact of encouragement, how can you be more intentional in offering genuine encouragement to those in your life? Are there specific individuals God is placing on your heart to encourage today?

7. **Prayer and Encouragement:** Spend some time in prayer, asking God to fill you with words of encouragement for others. Seek His

guidance on how to be an embodiment of His encouragement in your community.

As you meditate on these questions and the message from the sermon, may your heart be stirred to both seek and offer encouragement, recognizing its divine power to change lives.

CHAPTER 22

Devotional: Cultivating the Soil of Your Heart

Scripture Reading: Matthew 13:1-9

Reflection: The parable of the sower emphasizes the condition of our hearts as we hear and receive the Word of God. Just as a farmer tends to the soil to ensure it's ready for planting, we too must tend to the soil of our hearts. Jesus highlights four types of soil: the hardened, the troubled, the distracted, and the open. Each represents a condition of our heart and our readiness to receive and nurture the gospel message.

Thought for the Day: Our heart's condition directly affects how we receive and nurture the Word of God. How are you tending to the soil of your heart?

Prayer: Lord, help me to assess the condition of my heart. Show me areas that need tilling, nourishment, or weed removal. Guide me in nurturing the seed of Your Word, that it may bear fruit in my life. Amen.

Study Questions for Personal or Group Reflection:

1. **Reflection on the Soil Types:**

   - Which of the four types of soil do you identify with the most at this point in your life? Why?

   - Can you recall a time when your heart resembled each type of soil? What were the circumstances and outcomes?

2. **The Power of the Word:**

   - How has the power of the Word changed or shaped your life?

   - How do you prioritize the Word in your daily routine?

3. **Nurturing Growth:**

   - How do distractions in your life impact your relationship with God?

   - What "weeds" are currently present in your life that might be hindering your spiritual growth?

4. **Taking Action:**

   - What practical steps can you take this week to strengthen and nourish the soil of your heart?

   - How can you help others in cultivating their hearts for the gospel?

5. **The Role of the Holy Spirit:**

   - How do you recognize the prompting of the Holy Spirit in your life when it comes to nurturing the seed of the Word?

   - How can you partner with the Holy Spirit to ensure your heart remains fertile and receptive?

6. **Impact on Others:**

- How has the growth of the Word in your life impacted those around you?

- How can you be a sower of the Word, planting seeds in the lives of others?

As you reflect on these questions, consider journaling your answers. This will help solidify your commitments and track your spiritual growth over time. The parable of the sower is a reminder that our heart's condition is crucial. It's an ongoing journey of ensuring our heart remains open and receptive to God's Word, leading to transformation and abundant fruitfulness.

Dive Deeper Daily:

Day 1: Understanding the Parable

Scripture: Matthew 13:1-9

Devotional: In this parable, Jesus speaks about the Sower, the Seed, and the Soil. Understanding that the sower is Jesus and all believers who spread the gospel, and the seed is the Word of God, we can deduce that the seed is powerful and life-changing. The soil, on the other hand, is the heart of a person. The outcome of the seed depends heavily on the type of soil it lands on.

Questions for Reflection:

1. What does it mean to you that the seed, the Word of God, has power?

2. Why do you think Jesus chose to use the analogy of a sower, seed, and soil to describe the spread of the gospel?

Day 2: Recognizing a Hardened Heart

Scripture: Matthew 13:3-4

Devotional: A hardened heart does not allow the seed to penetrate and grow. While the seed is powerful, the soil must be receptive. The enemy often tries to snatch away the Word before it can take root in a person's life.

Questions for Reflection:

1. Have you ever felt like your heart was hardened to the gospel? Why?

2. What distractions or life events can lead to a heart becoming hardened?

Day 3: The Troubles of a Shallow Heart

Scripture: Matthew 13:5

Devotional: A heart that lacks depth, or a troubled heart, can be quick to receive the Word but may not sustain it through trials. It is essential to nurture and grow deep roots to withstand life's challenges.

Questions for Reflection:

1. Can you recall a time when you felt enthusiastic about your faith, but then wavered during difficulties?

2. What steps can you take to ensure your faith has deep roots?

Day 4: Avoiding a Distracted Heart

Scripture: Matthew 13:6-7

Devotional: Distractions can choke the growth of the seed in our hearts. Worldly desires and neglect can prevent the seed from bearing fruit. To see growth, we must prioritize and nurture our relationship with God.

Questions for Reflection:

1. What distractions in your life may be preventing spiritual growth?

2. How can you minimize or eliminate these distractions?

Day 5: Cultivating an Open Heart

Scripture: Matthew 13:8-9

Devotional: An open heart is one that receives the Word of God readily and nurtures it to bear fruit. This heart not only grows for itself but also impacts those around it positively.

Questions for Reflection:

1. What does having an open heart mean to you?

2. How can you ensure your heart remains open to the Word of God?

Day 6: The Result of a Healthy Heart

Devotional: A heart that is rooted in the Word of God can bear fruit, provide shade, nourish others, and spread seeds that lead to more growth. It's an ongoing cycle of blessings.

Questions for Reflection:

1. How have you witnessed the "fruits" of a heart rooted in the Word in your life or the lives of others?

2. How can you further cultivate your heart to produce more spiritual fruits?

Day 7: Nurturing Your Heart's Soil

Devotional: Your heart's soil condition is crucial for the growth of the gospel seed. Spending time in prayer, removing distractions, and dedicating time to the Word can help strengthen and nurture your heart's soil.

Questions for Reflection:

1. Which practices can you incorporate this week to fortify the soil of your heart?

2. How might dedicating regular time to God transform your relationship with Him?

As we journey through this week, let's strive to understand our hearts better and work towards creating an environment where the seed of the gospel can flourish.

CHAPTER 23

Devotional: Cultivating Spiritual Growth

Scripture Reading: Matthew 13:1-9

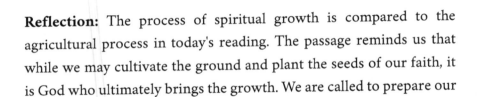

Reflection: The process of spiritual growth is compared to the agricultural process in today's reading. The passage reminds us that while we may cultivate the ground and plant the seeds of our faith, it is God who ultimately brings the growth. We are called to prepare our hearts, creating fertile ground for God's word to take root and flourish.

In our lives, we play a crucial role in our spiritual growth by regularly engaging with God's Word, immersing ourselves in a community of believers, dedicating time to prayer and worship, and consistently evaluating our lives against Christ's teachings. Yet, while these actions set the stage for growth, the transformation itself is a work of God's hand.

Moreover, we must remember that growth doesn't always come easy. Sometimes, our growth is through adversity. Like plants that face the wind and rain and come out stronger, our faith, too, becomes more robust through trials, making us more like Christ.

Prayer: Dear Heavenly Father, thank you for your unwavering love and grace. Help us to cultivate a heart receptive to Your Word and to recognize Your hand in our spiritual growth. Through seasons of joy and adversity, may we always remain rooted in You. Amen.

Study Questions:

1. In what ways can you cultivate fertile ground in your heart for God's word to flourish?

2. How can you actively involve yourself in a community that fosters spiritual growth?

3. Reflect on a time when you experienced spiritual growth through adversity. What did you learn from that season?

4. How does understanding that God is the one who brings about spiritual growth change your perspective on your spiritual journey?

5. Why is it crucial to continuously evaluate our spiritual life against the teachings of Christ?

6. How can you ensure that you are creating the right environment for spiritual growth in your life?

7. Paul emphasized the importance of focusing on God and not on human leaders or methods for growth. How can you ensure that your focus remains on God in your spiritual journey?

8. What are some "seasons of adversity" you've experienced or are experiencing? How can you see them as opportunities for growth?

Application: This week, dedicate some time each day to reflect on your spiritual growth journey. Assess the environment you've placed yourself in and make any necessary changes to ensure it's conducive to growth. Dive deeper into the Word, pray for guidance, and actively seek community that encourages your spiritual maturity. Remember always that while you plant and water, it is God who brings the growth.

Dive Deeper Daily:

Scripture: Matthew 13:1-9 (CEV)

Reflection: Spiritual growth, like the growth of plants, is a natural process but requires our cooperation. We must cultivate our hearts, prepare the soil, and plant the Word. It's not about our effort but about our openness to God's workings. Just as a farmer tills, plants, and waters the soil, we must do our part in the spiritual journey. However, the transformation and growth that happens is exclusively by God's power and design.

Today's Points to Ponder:

1. **Know the Source**: Remember, it's God who brings growth. We might have mentors, pastors, and leaders who help guide us, but it's God who changes our hearts.

2. **Embrace the Expectation**: God desires for us to grow. Being stagnant isn't what He has planned for us. We should always seek to move forward, leaving behind immaturity and embracing spiritual maturity.

3. **Seek the Right Environment**: We can't expect growth if we're constantly surrounding ourselves with negativity or sin. Just as a plant needs the right conditions to grow, so do our souls.

4. **Embrace Adversity**: Growth isn't always comfortable. Sometimes, our biggest growth spurts in faith come from the most challenging times in our lives.

Study Questions:

1. **Knowing the Source**:

   - Have you ever found yourself giving too much credit to a human instrument in your spiritual journey, rather than God?

   - What steps can you take to ensure that you always recognize God as the primary source of your growth?

2. **Embracing Expectation**:

   - Do you feel like you've been spiritually stagnant? If so, why?

   - What are some ways you can actively pursue growth in your faith?

3. **Seeking the Right Environment**:

   - Assess your current "spiritual environment." What aspects of your life encourage spiritual growth, and which ones hinder it?

   - How can you make changes to ensure you're in an environment conducive to growth?

4. **Embracing Adversity**:

- Reflect on a time of adversity in your life. How did it shape your relationship with God?

- How can you better prepare yourself spiritually for future challenges?

Prayer: Dear Heavenly Father, thank You for being the true source of our growth. Help us to always turn to You, to prepare our hearts, and to cultivate our souls so they are ready for Your transformative work. Give us the strength to persevere through adversity, knowing that it often leads to greater spiritual maturity. In Jesus' name, we pray. Amen.

CHAPTER 24

Devotional: "Growth in Connection"

Scripture Reading: John 15:1-5

Reflection: Many of us find ourselves striving for growth. In our careers, our relationships, and especially in our spiritual lives. However, growth isn't just about adding more – sometimes, it involves subtraction.

Jesus teaches us this concept in John 15, using the analogy of a vine and its branches. Just as a gardener prunes branches to stimulate growth and fruitfulness, God sometimes removes things from our lives to help us grow spiritually. This concept might seem counterintuitive, but it's a principle seen throughout Scripture.

For growth to happen, we need two things: the right foundation and the right connection. The Word of God is our foundation – it's the root system that sustains and nurtures us. Jesus is our connection – the true vine that provides everything we need to thrive.

As we abide in Him, drawing sustenance and life from our connection to the vine, we begin to bear fruit. Not just any fruit, but the fruit of the Spirit: love, joy, peace, patience, kindness, goodness, faithfulness, gentleness, and self-control. When we see these qualities increasing in our lives, we know we're truly connected to the vine.

Reflection:

- What things might God be asking you to subtract from your life to help you grow?

- How can you strengthen your connection to Jesus, the true vine, today?

Study Questions:

1. **Identifying the True Vine:** How does Jesus identify Himself in John 15:1? Why is this identification significant in the context of Old Testament prophecies and the Jewish audience of His time?

2. **The Role of the Gardener:** What role does the Father, the gardener, play in the growth and fruitfulness of the branches?

3. **Purpose of Pruning:** Why is pruning necessary for a plant's growth and fruitfulness? How does this relate to spiritual growth in a believer's life?

4. **The Importance of Abiding:** What does it mean to "abide" in Jesus according to John 15:4-5? Why is it crucial for a believer to remain connected to the vine?

5. **Characteristics of Fruit:** Based on the sermon, what are the three characteristics of fruit? How do these characteristics reflect a believer's relationship with Jesus?

6. **Growth and Maturity:** Reflect on the progression from "no fruit" to "fruit" to "more fruit" and finally to "much fruit" as described in the sermon. How does this progression mirror your own spiritual journey?

7. **Personal Reflection:** Can you identify areas in your life where you have experienced "addition by subtraction"? How did these moments of pruning lead to growth and fruitfulness in your relationship with God?

Remember, growth often involves subtraction before addition. As we remain connected to Jesus, our source of life and sustenance, we can trust that the Gardener knows exactly what He's doing. Even when we don't understand the pruning process, we can be sure it's for our ultimate good and His glory.

Dive Deeper Daily:

Day 1 – The True Vine

Scripture Reading: John 15:1-5

Devotional Message: In our walk with God, we may face challenges and struggles, but we can always remember that Jesus is our True Vine. In Him, we find our strength, our nourishment, and our very life. When we stay connected to Him, we can bear much fruit.

Reflection: Consider the ways in which you are staying connected to Jesus, the True Vine. Are there areas in your life where you feel disconnected? What steps can you take to remain rooted in Him?

Study Questions:

1. How does the image of the vine and branches illustrate our relationship with Jesus?

2. What are the consequences of being disconnected from the vine?

3. How can you ensure you remain connected to the True Vine daily?

Daily Devotional: Day 2 – Pruning for Growth

Scripture Reading: John 15:1-5

Devotional Message: Growth often requires subtraction. Just as a gardener prunes the branches to help the plant grow more fruitfully, God sometimes removes things from our lives to help us grow spiritually. While it may be painful at the moment, it is essential for our spiritual growth.

Reflection: Think about a time in your life when you felt God was "pruning" something away. How did it result in growth or a deeper relationship with Him?

Study Questions:

1. Why is pruning necessary for a plant's health and fruitfulness?

2. How can pruning be seen as an act of love and care?

3. Are there things in your life right now that may need pruning for spiritual growth?

Daily Devotional: Day 3 – Abiding in Christ

Scripture Reading: John 15:1-5

Devotional Message: To abide means to remain or stay. As branches, we are called to remain in Christ, drawing our strength, sustenance, and vitality from Him. By staying close to Jesus, we can bear fruit that reflects His character.

Reflection: In what practical ways do you abide in Christ daily? How do you cultivate a deeper relationship with Him?

Study Questions:

1. What does it mean to "abide" in Christ?

2. How can you tell if someone is abiding in Christ by their actions or character?

3. What challenges do you face in abiding in Christ, and how can you overcome them?

Daily Devotional: Day 4 – Bearing Fruit

Scripture Reading: John 15:1-5

Devotional Message: The fruit we bear as Christians should reflect the nature and character of Jesus. It's not just for us but benefits others and brings glory to God. By abiding in Christ, we can produce love, joy, peace, and all the fruits of the Spirit.

Reflection: Reflect on the fruits of the Spirit mentioned in Galatians 5:22-23. Which fruits are most evident in your life? Which do you need to cultivate more?

Study Questions:

1. How does abiding in Christ relate to bearing fruit?

2. Why is it important for our fruit to benefit others?

3. Which fruits of the Spirit do you feel you need to focus on developing more, and why?

Daily Devotional: Day 5 – Shout Hallelujah

Scripture Reading: John 15:1-5

Devotional Message: Recognizing the growth and transformation in our lives should lead us to a place of gratitude and praise. Remembering where God has brought us from and seeing the fruit He has cultivated in us calls for a shout of "Hallelujah!"

Reflection: Reflect on your journey with Christ. Where has He brought you from? How has He transformed your life?

Study Questions:

1. Why is it important to recognize and celebrate spiritual growth?

2. How has the fruit of the Spirit become more evident in your life over time?

3. How can you share your testimony of growth and transformation with others?

Remember, the purpose of these devotionals is to encourage deeper reflection on God's Word, challenge you in your faith, and promote growth in your relationship with Christ. Take time each day to read the scripture, ponder the message, and answer the questions honestly and thoughtfully.

CHAPTER 25

Devotional: "Harvest Time: Trust the Process"

Scripture Reading: 2 Corinthians 9:6-10

Reflection: The principle of sowing and reaping is foundational in farming, but it is also a divine principle that guides our lives. When we think about harvests, we often anticipate the blessings and breakthroughs. Yet, as the sermon reminds us, for every harvest, there's a required season of planting.

For believers, sowing isn't just an act but a lifestyle. Our daily choices, actions, and words are seeds that we plant, and in time, they will yield their harvest. The scripture emphasizes that if we sow generously, we reap generously. This mirrors the unconditional and overwhelming love God has for us. As we're rooted in Him and as we allow the fruits of the Spirit to manifest in our lives, we're sowing seeds that lead to a transformative harvest.

However, the journey to the harvest isn't always instantaneous. Between sowing and reaping, there are seasons of waiting, growth, and even pruning. While these seasons might be challenging, they're crucial for the full development and maturation of our harvest. The wait might seem long, but God is always at work, even when it feels like He's silent.

Today, be encouraged to trust the process of the harvest. Even if you don't see immediate results, know that God is working behind the scenes to bring about a bountiful harvest in His perfect timing.

Reflection:

1. **Seed Planting**: Reflect on the seeds you've been planting in your life. Are they seeds that will yield the fruit of the Spirit or seeds of negativity, hate, or chaos?

2. **Trust in God's Timing**: Think about a time you grew impatient waiting for a "harvest" in your life. How can you remind yourself of God's perfect timing in such moments?

3. **Seasons of Life**: Ecclesiastes 3 speaks about different seasons. What season do you feel you are in right now? How can you make the most of this current season?

Prayer: Dear Heavenly Father, thank You for the principle of sowing and reaping. Help me to sow good seeds in my life and trust Your timing for the harvest. Even in moments of impatience or doubt, remind me that You're always at work. I pray for the grace to trust the process, knowing that every season has its purpose. Amen.

Study Questions:

1. **Understanding Sowing and Reaping**: How does the principle of sowing and reaping apply to areas of your life beyond farming or gardening?

2. **The Fruit of the Spirit**: Which fruit of the Spirit do you find most evident in your life? Which one do you struggle with the most?

3. **The Waiting Season**: How can we find strength and perseverance during the waiting seasons of our lives? Are there any scriptures or promises from God that you hold onto during these times?

4. **Repentance as Resowing**: The sermon mentions repentance as a way to "resow". What does this mean to you? How can one effectively "resow" after realizing they've planted undesirable seeds in their life?

5. **Connection to Christ**: Reflect on John 15:5. How does staying connected to Christ influence the kind of harvest we receive? How can one cultivate a stronger connection with Christ?

Dive into these questions, and allow them to help you internalize the message of the sermon and the principle of sowing and reaping in your own life. It's a principle that, when understood and applied, can lead to transformation, growth, and abundant blessings.

Dive Deeper Daily:

Day 1: Planting Seeds of Faith

Scripture Reading: 2 Corinthians 9:6

Reflection: Just as a farmer cannot expect a harvest without planting seeds, we too cannot expect blessings without putting in the effort.

Many want the results without putting in the work, but spiritual growth and blessings come from consistently sowing seeds of faith, love, and hope.

Study Questions:

1. What seeds are you planting in your spiritual life?

2. How does the anticipation of a harvest motivate you in your spiritual journey?

3. What prevents you from sowing regularly?

Day 2: Quantity and Quality of Sowing

Scripture Reading: Luke 6:38 and Galatians 5:22-23

Reflection: The amount and type of seed you sow determines the harvest you'll reap. As believers, we are called to sow abundantly and sow good seeds. When we sow seeds of the Spirit, we can expect to reap a harvest rich in love, joy, peace, patience, and other fruits of the Spirit.

Study Questions:

1. What are some tangible ways you can sow generously in your life?

2. Reflect on the fruits of the Spirit. Which one do you need to cultivate more?

3. How does knowing the potential harvest impact your sowing?

Day 3: The Results of What You Sow

Scripture Reading: Galatians 6:7-8

Reflection: Our actions have consequences, and the Bible cautions us not to be deceived. If we sow to please our flesh, we will reap destruction. However, sowing to please the Spirit brings eternal rewards.

Study Questions:

1. How can you shift from sowing to please the flesh to sowing to please the Spirit?

2. Are there areas in your life where you've seen the direct consequences of your sowing?

3. What does repentance (resowing) look like in your life?

Day 4: Staying Connected to Christ

Scripture Reading: John 15:5

Reflection: To bear good fruit, we must remain in Christ. Staying connected to Him is the secret to a bountiful harvest. It's not just about sowing but sowing in Christ.

Study Questions:

1. How do you remain connected to Christ daily?

2. What challenges do you face in maintaining this connection?

3. Reflect on a time when being connected to Christ produced noticeable fruit in your life.

Day 5: Trusting the Harvest Process

Scripture Reading: Galatians 6:9 and Ecclesiastes 3:1-2

Reflection: Just as there's a season for planting and a season for harvesting, in our spiritual journey, there's a time for sowing and a time for reaping. We must be patient and trust God's timing, even when we can't see the immediate results.

Study Questions:

1. How do you cope when you don't see immediate results from your efforts?

2. How does understanding the different seasons of life help you maintain patience and hope?

3. Reflect on a past season where you saw the fruits of your labor. What did you learn from that season?

Day 6: The Work Continues

Scripture Reading: Philippians 1:6

Reflection: The good news is, even when we stumble or face obstacles, God continues His work in us. The seeds of the word have been planted in our hearts, and God ensures it grows and bears fruit.

Study Questions:

1. How do you feel knowing that God continues to work in you despite your shortcomings?

2. Reflect on a time when you felt God's refining process in your life.

3. What steps can you take to cooperate more with God's work in your life?

Day 7: Embracing the Harvest Time

Reflection: As we wrap up the week, let's remember that the harvest time is both a celebration and a call to action. For some, it's a call to accept the gift of salvation; for others, it's an invitation to embrace the fruits of their labor in Christ.

Study Questions:

1. How will you celebrate the spiritual harvest in your life?

2. In what ways can you share the fruits of your spiritual harvest with others?

3. Reflect and thank God for the seeds He has allowed you to plant and the harvest you are witnessing in your life.

CHAPTER 26

Devotional: "The Process of Harvest"

Scripture Reading: John 4:1-42

Reflection: The narrative in John 4 tells a powerful tale about recognizing the harvest right in front of us. When we talk about the harvest, we don't just mean the blessings we receive but the souls waiting to be touched by the love of God. The story of Jesus and the Samaritan woman serves as a reminder that every interaction can lead to transformation.

Key Points:

1. **The Process**: Harvesting isn't an overnight event. It's a series of stages that require faith, patience, and divine intervention. It's about believing in the unseen, trusting in God's timing, and remembering the journey from seed to fruit.

2. **Breaking Barriers**: Jesus, by initiating conversation with the Samaritan woman, broke societal norms and barriers. It's a

reminder for us that sometimes, our harvest lies in unfamiliar territories or with those whom society might overlook.

3. **Living Water**: When Jesus spoke of the living water, He offered eternal satisfaction. The world offers temporary pleasures, but the water Jesus provides quenches our spiritual thirst forever.

4. **Recognizing the Harvest**: Blessings aren't always grandiose; sometimes, they're the simple things we take for granted. Moreover, our spiritual harvest — souls waiting for the love and truth of Christ — are all around us.

Study Questions:

1. **Personal Reflection**: Can you recall a time in your life where you witnessed the process of a blessing unfolding? What stages did you recognize from seed to harvest?

2. **Barrier Breakdown**: Are there barriers or prejudices that might be preventing you from seeing the harvest in front of you? What steps can you take to break these barriers?

3. **Living Water**: In what ways have you experienced the 'living water' that Jesus offers? How does it differ from the temporary satisfactions of the world?

4. **Counting Blessings**: List down five 'small' blessings you're grateful for today. How do they contribute to your daily joy and contentment?

5. **Eyes on the Harvest**: Think of people in your life who might be part of your 'spiritual harvest.' How can you reach out and share the love of Christ with them?

6. **Active Faith**: How can you be an active laborer in the harvest? Are there specific actions or commitments you can make to ensure you're playing your part in the Kingdom's work?

Prayer: Dear Heavenly Father, we thank you for the process of the harvest, for the blessings both big and small. Help us to recognize the opportunities around us, to break barriers, and to be laborers for your Kingdom. Quench our thirst with your living water, and let us be vessels to share it with others. In Jesus' name, Amen.

Dive Deeper Daily:

Day 1: Recognizing the Process

Scripture: John 4:34-35

Reflection: The journey from seed to harvest is a beautiful metaphor for our spiritual growth. Just like a seed transforms into a fruit, we too evolve in our walk with God.

Study Questions:

1. Can you identify a situation where you witnessed a transformation, either in yourself or someone else?

2. What role did faith play in this transformation?

Day 2: Celebrating the Growth

Reflection: Every stage in the process holds significance. Remembering where we started makes the harvest even sweeter.

Study Questions:

1. Reflect on your personal journey with God. Can you identify the different stages?

2. How do you celebrate your spiritual growth?

Day 3: Water is Essential

Reflection: Jesus offered the Samaritan woman living water, a metaphor for spiritual sustenance. We too require spiritual nourishment to grow.

Study Questions:

1. How do you nourish your spirit?

2. Can you recall a time when someone unexpectedly offered you spiritual or emotional refreshment?

Day 4: The Son Exposes

Reflection: Jesus, the light of the world, has a way of revealing truths in our lives. With Him, we can confront and heal our sins.

Study Questions:

1. Reflect on a time when you felt spiritually enlightened after an encounter with Jesus.

2. How do you cope when faced with uncomfortable truths about yourself?

Day 5: Embrace Immediate Harvest

Reflection: Blessings are often right in front of us. However, sometimes we're too focused on the future that we overlook them.

Study Questions:

1. List down the small blessings you've experienced today.

2. Why do you think we often overlook the immediate blessings in pursuit of bigger ones?

Day 6: The Spiritual Harvest

Reflection: Beyond the material world, there's a spiritual harvest of souls yearning for God's love. These are the overlooked and undervalued in society.

Study Questions:

1. How can you play a part in bringing the 'Samaritans' of today closer to God?

2. Reflect on a time when you felt led to share God's love with someone. What was the outcome?

Day 7: Laborers in the Harvest

Reflection: While the harvest is abundant, workers are few. We are called to join God in His work, to reach out to those around us.

Study Questions:

1. In what ways can you be a laborer in God's harvest?

2. Why do you think many are hesitant to join in the work, despite the plentiful harvest?

Closing Prayer: Lord, as we walk with You, open our eyes to the harvest around us. Fill us with living water, nourish our souls, and guide us to share Your love with those in need. Teach us to celebrate every growth, every transformation, and every blessing – big or small. In Jesus' name, we pray. Amen.

Closing Chapter

The Bible, in its timeless tapestry, invites us not just to read, but to commune. It is not merely a book to be studied, but a relationship to be nurtured. The pages we've turned, the verses we've pondered, have opened our eyes and hearts to the boundless realm of God's love—a love that transcends time, space, and human understanding.

Through our personal study, we've embarked on a journey deep within, exploring the caverns of our souls, and further still, into the divine heart. Each scripture, when applied personally, becomes a living testament, a testament of God's intimate involvement in our lives. The stories of old are not tales of distant times; they echo the sentiments, struggles, and triumphs of our own lives.

In the face of challenges, we've found solace in the Psalms; in moments of doubt, we've sought clarity in the Proverbs; and in times of despair, we've clung to the promises of Revelation. With every application of scripture to our personal lives, we've not only deepened our understanding of the text but have also unraveled layers of God's ceaseless love for us.

For love is the very essence of the Bible. It's the thread that weaves through every story, every prophecy, every admonition. And it's in our personal encounters with this love, through dedicated study and application, that we begin to grasp its profound depth. Like a well with no bottom, God's love offers new discoveries, new insights, and new revelations with every descent.

As we draw this book to a close, let us remember that our journey with the Bible is eternal. Its wisdom is inexhaustible, its truths, immutable. The Word beckons us to return, time and again, to drink from its well, to immerse ourselves in its teachings, and to let its verses illuminate our path.

Though this chapter ends, our exploration does not. The Bible, a reservoir of divine love, remains forever open to us, offering fresh insights, new understandings, and deeper connections with every reading. So, let us continue to study, to reflect, and to apply. For in doing so, we don't just uncover the words of a book, but the heartbeat of the Creator—a heartbeat that resonates with love, for you and for all. I leave you with a timeless truth: the Bible is not just a testament of God's love; it's an invitation to experience it, personally and profoundly.

Made in the USA
Columbia, SC
21 May 2024

35582867R20087